Praise for *The Happy, Healthy Nonprofit*

"*The Happy, Healthy Nonprofit* is an essential guide for leaders and organizations looking to make a positive social impact on their communities and all around the world. Beth Kanter and Aliza Sherman lay out a clear and compelling case for building sustainable lives while changing the world."

—Arianna Huffington, *Huffington Post*

"Many social good activists who leverage the power of spreading good through small acts are passionate about whatever they are trying to change in the world. That passion, however, is a double-edged sword: it propels them forward, but often comes at the expense of their health and happiness. Kanter/Sherman's book shows how these passionate individuals can incorporate self-care and well-being into their lives in order to sustain that work. A must-read."

—Jennifer Aaker, General Atlantic Professor of Marketing at Stanford University's Graduate School of Business.

"I'm entering my second decade as an executive coach and an instructor at the Stanford Graduate School of Business. *The Happy, Healthy Nonprofit* covers many of the same topics that I discuss with business leaders and MBA students and write about for the *Harvard Business Review*. Beth and her coauthor Aliza Sherman have created an essential resource for every nonprofit professional."

—Ed Batista, Executive Coach and Instructor, Stanford Graduate School of Business

"For too long, we have lamented the heroic leadership and martyrdom prevalent in nonprofits without actually proposing an alternate way of operationalizing a commitment to staff well-being. Beth Kanter and Aliza Sherman finally take this on. Starting from their personal stories of recommitting to their own well-being and then drawing in the expertise of others, they offer practical strategies for prioritizing wellness. Organizations can no longer ignore this mandate!"

—Jeanne Bell, CompassPoint

"As an advocate for thriving in one's work and life, I recommend *The Happy, Healthy Nonprofit* as an essential guide for social change leaders and organizations looking to make a positive impact on their communities and world. Beth Kanter and Aliza Sherman lay out a clear and compelling case not just for self-care for individuals but also a 'WE-care' culture shift for organizations to create happier, healthier workplaces."

—Heather L. Carpenter, Coauthor of *The Talent Development Platform: Putting People First in Social Change Organizations*

"Doing work that matters is rarely easy. Aliza and Beth have written a book that doesn't shy away from this. It is truthful, honest, and fun while motivating you not to give up and to keep doing your important work. It doesn't matter if you run the largest foundation in the world or are volunteering on weekends. This book will inspire you to take better care of yourself so you can do your work in a more healthy and sustainable way."

—C.C. Chapman, Author of *Amazing Things Will Happen: A Real-World Guide on Achieving Success and Happiness*

"Many dream of a life of service and then are surprised at the strain this work can cause both emotionally and physically. While we know intellectually that we cannot fully give ourselves to others if we do not take care of ourselves, our passion for our work, the heavy emotional investment it requires, and our organizations' limited resources can combine to take a personal toll. In *The Happy, Healthy Nonprofit*, Beth Kanter and Aliza Sherman shine a light on this challenge, giving us practical tools for self-care and for creating the kind of organizational health that's needed if we and our co-workers are going to have the endurance, the perseverance, and the joy required to make lasting change."

—Sasha Dichter, Chief Innovation Officer, Acumen

"As a nonprofit leader for decades, I know how easy it is to give so much to your cause that you deplete yourself. In *The Happy, Healthy Nonprofit,* Beth Kanter and Aliza Sherman provide an essential guide to elevate self-care as a strategic tool for nonprofit professionals who want to perform at their best as they work to change the world."

—Gloria Feldt, Cofounder and President, Take The Lead, and author of *No Excuses: 9 Ways Women Can Change How We Think About Power*

"*The Happy, Healthy Nonprofit* reframes 'work' not as the drudgery that leaves most of us broken and burned out, but as a vehicle for meaning, well-being, and happiness. It is a smart guide that offers practical and important strategies for integrating self-care into the fabric of organizations. *The Happy, Healthy Nonprofit* is a must-read for every person in every nonprofit organization from the board room to the C-suite to the staff and the interns. Read it. Mark it up. Turn down the pages. Share it. Do it."

—Allison Fine, Author, *Matterness: Fearless Leadership for a Social World*

"The 'put on your own oxygen mask first before helping others' message from the airlines could not be more relevant to the nonprofit sector and brought to life by this book. This is an essential read for the extraordinary nonprofit and social change leaders around the world working tirelessly to serve our communities. Thanks to Beth and Aliza—both for writing this and leading by example in their own professional lives."

—Meg Garlinghouse, Head of LinkedIn for Good

"A much needed guide for nonprofits to meet their employees and volunteers where they are, and a handy tool for anyone looking to sustain a demanding mission-focused career. Beth Kanter and Aliza Sherman serve as our self-care docents, and their book feels as much like a hug as a template for nonprofit workers who yearn for permission to take care of themselves while still being dedicated to their mission."

—Wendy Harman, White House Presidential Innovation Fellow

"We NGO types are a pretty righteous bunch. I mean, I spend my time working to end all sorts of global ills that have plagued the earth since the dawn of time—poverty, hunger, horrible diseases. And the thinking goes 'because they suffer, I must too.' When someone leaves the office early, the running joke (with a bite) is 'you are letting poverty win!' Beth and Aliza are offering a guidebook to save us from ourselves."

—Tom Hart, Executive Director, North America, the ONE Campaign

"There is no problem more pressing in the social sector than the burning out of the best and brightest talent in our field—we cannot be of service to our communities if we have driven ourselves into the ground. What a blessing to have great minds like Beth Kanter and Aliza Sherman on the case to encourage us all to help ourselves, our organizations, and our future."

—Clayton Lord, Vice President of Local Arts Advancement, Americans for the Arts

"You're no good to the cause if you're not being good to yourself. *The Happy, Healthy Nonprofit* is a much needed guide to help get the most out of the human element in an organization."

—Steven R. MacLaughlin, Director of Analytics, Blackbaud, Inc.

"The only asset we have for making a contribution to the world is ourselves. Yet so many well-intended social entrepreneurs forget this and burn out. Good motives are not enough: we need the kind of practical wisdom on offer in every page of this book from Beth and Aliza!"

—Greg McKeown, New York Times Bestselling Author of *Essentialism: The Disciplined Pursuit of Less.*

"It's common for passionate social change leaders to throw themselves into their work, while neglecting to take care of themselves: we all know people and organizations that have burned out from these bad habits. But if we want to create sustained social impact at scale—and high-performing nonprofits—then we need to focus more on personal and organizational sustainability. And as Gandhi so wisely counseled, we must be the change we want to see in the world. Luckily Kanter and Sherman give us invaluable advice on how to redefine our approach toward work, create healthy organizational cultures, and pursue our passions with purpose and joy."

—Heather McLeod Grant, Coauthor of the best-selling *Forces for Good*, and social impact adviser

Pacing oneself for marathon weeks versus sprint days is a vital lesson for nonprofit leaders to learn. *The Happy, Healthy Nonprofit: Strategies for Impact Without Burnout* should be read by all nonprofit leaders who thrive on adrenalin but who know they need more than just the coffee buzz to lead an effective organization. Beth Kanter and Aliza Sherman provide common sense information in an actionable way. The time is now to make this personal commitment to ourselves, each other, and the communities we serve.

—Kim Meredith, Executive Director, Stanford Center on Philanthropy and Civil Society, Stanford Social Innovation Review

"No one works harder than a nonprofit professional—funder driven stress, lack of resources, and work/life balance are challenges constantly faced by those working to make the world a better place. *The Happy, Healthy Nonprofit* is a must-read for leaders of organisations both great and small, who want to transform, support, and grow their social good missions."

—Carlos Miranda, Founder of I.G. Advisors and Social Misfits Media

"At a time when the lines between 'work' and 'life' are becoming more blurry, emerging leaders are seeking new ways to lead a fulfilling social good career. Beth Kanter and Aliza Sherman have created a must-have guide that champions self-care for individuals and organizations so they can thrive while doing good in the world. This book gives critical advice on building a happier, healthier nonprofit culture that will attract and retain young talent in the sector, addressing many of the challenges young nonprofit professionals face in the workplace."

—Amber Cruz Mohring, Co-Executive Director, YNPN

"Great nonprofits create a culture of well-being in their workplaces that encourages self-care because they know that their people are mission critical. Beth Kanter and Aliza Sherman have created a must-have guide that champions self-care for individuals and organizations in the nonprofit sector."

—Perla Ni, Great Nonprofits

"Beth Kanter and Aliza Sherman compellingly address the challenges and opportunities of the millennial generation by shining a light on the importance of self-care. *The Happy,*

Healthy Nonprofit can, should, and will start an important well-being movement in the nonprofit sector to become a better workplace for all! It is a must-read for anyone who sees themselves as a leader in the sector!"

—Yaniv Rivlin, Senior Program Officer, Charles and Lynn Schusterman Family Foundation

"In *The Happy, Healthy Nonprofit*, Beth and Aliza teach us that employee wellness and organizational performance are not only directly correlated but causal. Investing time and prioritizing effort in keeping the most valuable asset a nonprofit organization has— its people—both happy and healthy is an effective strategy to keeping the organization high-performing."

—Ettore Rossetti, Sr. Director, Social Business Strategy & Innovation, Save the Children; 2015 AMA Nonprofit Marketer of the Year; Two-time Guinness World Records® Title Holder

"As social entrepreneurs we can't make an impact in changing other people's lives unless we attend to our well-being. *The Happy, Healthy Nonprofit* is an essential guide for social change leaders and organizations who need to take care of themselves while seeking to make a positive change in the world."

—Premal Shah, President and Co-Founder, Kiva.Org

"By encouraging us to extend our heartfelt values, often directed only at our missions, to the people and teams that drive them, there is no doubt in my mind that *The Happy, Healthy Nonprofit* is an essential tool and a must-read for all those involved in the social impact sector dedicated to a life of meaning and purpose to create a better world."

—Kyla Shawyer, CEO, The Resource Alliance

"Regular followers of social media mavens Beth Kanter and Aliza Sherman will marvel at the way they balance intense and productive careers with caring and creative home lives. Now the rest of us can learn the secrets of how they found balance in their personal and professional lives in their new book, *The Happy, Healthy Nonprofit*."

—Vincent Stehle, Executive Director, Media Impact Funders

"Beth Kanter and Aliza Sherman have committed personally and professionally to the success of the nonprofit sector and the social change leaders who work tirelessly to do good in the world. Their guide to caring for ourselves, our people, and our organizations is indispensable for anyone looking to achieve success and make an impact over the long term."

—Henry Timms, Executive Director, 92nd Street Y

"*The Happy, Healthy Nonprofit* is essential reading for everyone in the social sector. First and foremost, it provides a clear path to survival for those at the front lines of social change who experience the stress and strain of our passionate, but under-resourced sector on a daily basis. But in the long term, the book is a wake-up call for every leader, board member, and funder who doesn't understand the risk we have of losing incredible talent and the real price of burn out. Beth and Aliza have achieved a masterful feat—providing practical guidance and a call to action—all in one book!"

—Victoria Vrana, Senior Program Officer, Philanthropic Partnerships Team, Bill & Melinda Gates Foundation

"Admit it: you do this work because you care about others and making the world a better place. But somewhere along the way you forgot how to care for yourself and your colleagues. Worry not. Beth Kanter and Aliza Sherman get it and are here to help you and your organization to embrace not just self-care but WE-care."

—Suzanne Elise Walsh, Deputy Director, Postsecondary Success, Bill & Melinda Gates Foundation

THE
HAPPY,
HEALTHY
NONPROFIT

STRATEGIES FOR IMPACT WITHOUT BURNOUT

THE HAPPY, HEALTHY NONPROFIT

BETH KANTER ALIZA SHERMAN

WILEY

Cover image: © iStock.com/Pingwin
Cover design: Wiley

This book is printed on acid-free paper.

Published by John Wiley & Sons, Inc., Hoboken, New Jersey

Published simultaneously in Canada

ISBN 978-1-119-25111-8 (cloth)
ISBN 978-1-119-25112-5 (ePDF)
ISBN 978-1-119-25358-7 (ePub)

Printed in the United States of America

10 9 8 7 6 5 4 3 2 1

From Beth:
In memory of my dad, Dr. Earl Kanter.
To my family, Walter, Harry, and Sara.

From Aliza:
In memory of my dad, Retired Cdr. Myron B. Sherman.
To Greg, Noa Grace, and Josiah. Family.

Contents

Our Acknowledgments

Whenever you write a book, there are so many people who help make it possible. We want to start with thanking our book agent, Jessica Faust of BookEnds, LLC, and our tireless book assistant, Angeles Winesett. We also want to thank the entire team at John Wiley & Sons, including Matthew Davis, who started us out, Heather Brosius, Brian Neill, Jocelyn Kwiatkowski, Alyssa Benigno, and Shannon Vargo.

Special thanks to Vu Le of the *Nonprofit With Balls* blog for agreeing to write the Foreword to our book even while sleepless with a newborn. Tequila! A huge round of applause to Rob Cottingham, our talented cartoonist who made us snort our lattes when we received his sketches. And to Arianna Huffington for fighting for our right to sleep.

A big thank-you to the Alliance of the Nonprofit Management and Annie Hernandez for letting us facilitate a design lab at the conference as part of the research. And to Chrissie Bonner for her superb graphic facilitation. Thank you to Americans for the Arts and Clayton Lord and Laura Kakolewski for letting us facilitate a design lab with the leadership group at the National Arts Marketing Project Conference.

And our heartfelt thanks to the many amazing nonprofit professionals and experts who gave their time and shared their stories with us about burnout, self-care, and organizational culture.

This book is for everyone who is doing the hard work to make our world a better place.

BETH'S ACKNOWLEDGMENTS

I couldn't have worked on this book without the love and support from my family when I was at the computer writing or when I needed to take long walks to think about the book or for self-care. And I couldn't have written this book without Aliza Sherman who made working on the book project an exciting journey of curiosity, creativity, learning, and fun and shares my passion for magic markers and drawing. I know that with Aliza as a writing partner, I've become a better writer. But, more important, she helped break my 35-year habit of adding two spaces after periods!

ALIZA'S ACKNOWLEDGMENTS

I couldn't have worked on this book without patience and understanding from my family when my nose was stuck to my computer screen and my brain was in this book. And I couldn't have written this book without Beth Kanter who I've known for years and got to know even better in the past 12 months. Here's hoping her generosity of spirit, brilliance of mind, and dedication to walking has rubbed off on me. Here's to Oxford commas and finding our way out of rabbit holes!

Foreword

Okay, one more triple bacon-infused tequila. But I'm adding a kale garnish. Self-care!

When I got the e-mail from Beth and Aliza asking me to write this foreword, I nearly spit up a mouthful of tequila all over my keyboard. Stop judging; it had been a rough week, and that was my self-care tequila. I keep it under my desk, along with several bars of dark chocolate, and pull it out after getting grant rejections, receiving unfair criticisms from my board, or any time the phrase "annual gala" comes up at any meeting.

Honestly, asking me to write the foreword to a book on self-care is like asking my toddler to write the intro to *The Joys of Sharing Your Toys* or *No More Tantrums: Effective Communication with Your Parents*. Having been an executive director for over a decade, I have picked up some horrible habits, such as eating lunch at my desk while reading e-mails, staying up late working every night, and saying yes to every request of my time. I developed this one weird twitch in my left eye and started scaring staff and volunteers. The concept of self-care came along, and I scoffed, deciding that I would rather juggle mason jars full of live scorpions than do yoga or chug a green smoothie every morning, or bathe every day, or whatever this hippie philosophy entails.

But reading this book, the book in your hands, made me realize self-care is way more than the downward-facing dog and kale smoothies. Beth and Aliza, with their signature humor, piercing insight, and concrete advice, present a compelling argument for why we burn out and why it is important for all of us to take care of ourselves and each other and create happy, healthy, supportive environments in which to do our work.

A while ago, in a period of overwhelming stress, I wrote the Nonprofit Unicorn's Mantra:

> I am a nonprofit unicorn. I try each day to make the world better. I am good at some stuff, and I suck at some stuff, and that's okay. There's way more crap than I can possibly do on any given day. On some days I am more productive than on other days, and that's okay. I know sometimes there are things that I certainly could have done better. I know that I can't make everyone happy or spend as much time as I could on everyone. I know there's a bunch of crap I don't know. Sometimes I make mistakes, and that's okay. I will try my best to learn and to improve, but I'll also give myself a break. I will be as thoughtful and understanding with myself as I am with my coworkers and community members. I am an awesome and sexy nonprofit unicorn.

That mantra has carried me through some tough days as a nonprofit professional doing work I love. Beth and Aliza, though, made me realize self-care is not just about individuals but also about organizational culture and combatting sector-level philosophies such as scarcity and martyrdom, about changing unrealistic expectations and restrictions from funders and from society. The shift from self-care to WE-care, as discussed in this book, is a critical shift our sector must make if we want to effectively address the injustice and inequity facing our community every day.

It comes down to this: our work matters, but it is ongoing and we must sustain ourselves for the long run. Self-care is no longer just about us as individuals. Unlike many other professions that will likely be taken over by robots, human nonprofit professionals will always be needed due to the complexity of our work. We lift up families; we build communities. If we burn out, the cost to our world is high.

Thank you for all that you do. If you are reading this book, you are probably a nonprofit professional contributing to making the world a better, safer, happier place for me and my tantrum-throwing toddler. I am very grateful. I know our field is not easy, and, in fact, it can be maddening. But our work is vital, and it cannot be done without the amazing professionals dedicating untold hours every day to it. Please take care of yourself as you take care of others, and let's make every nonprofit a happy and healthy place, where our eyes don't twitch and where we can take swigs of Jose Cuervo simply for its exquisite flavor.

Vu Le
Nonprofitwithballs.com

Introduction

THE VISION

Cue up the Pharrell Williams song, "Happy."

It might seem crazy what we're about to say, but work-life balance is good when you can take a break. Clap along if you want to know what happy and healthy is to you. Clap along if you feel "happy and healthy nonprofits achieve results" is the truth.

Let's face it: your health and happiness directly affect how you feel at work and affect your productivity. Attending to your well-being can be the antidote to stress and prevention of burnout, and those are great reasons to start practicing self-care. According to the World Health Organization, self-care is "what people do for themselves to establish and maintain health, and to prevent and deal with illness."[1]

Working for a nonprofit that has limited resources can be a pressure cooker, but what if your organization's culture encouraged you, and everyone who worked there, to embrace self-care without guilt? What if you could feel the vibrancy of your organization when you stepped into the physical office or hear it in the voices of staff when they talked about what it is like to work at your organization? What if every time your organization advertised a position, you were flooded with exceptional applicants because of your nonprofit's reputation for a culture of well-being with policies and benefits to support it? Imagine the increase in results your organization would experience because of high talent retention rates instead of high turnover, eliminating cracks in your institutional memory.

What if this was *your* organization?

We've just described the *Happy, Healthy Nonprofit.* This book provides you and your organization with a road map to getting there—from creating a self-care plan for yourself to weaving well-being into the DNA of your nonprofit by developing and implementing a happy, healthy strategy.

In this book, we define "wellness" as traditional physical and mental health versus "well-being," a state of being comfortable, happy, and healthy that contributes to wellness. Workplace well-being goes beyond the typical lip service toward self-care such as distributing brochures about burnout or bringing in an occasional speaker to an all-staff meeting to talk about stress relief or nutrition. Offering the occasional massage on-site or giving staff a few paid hours off as a "reward" isn't a sustainable happy, healthy strategy.

When self-care initiatives are treated as extras instead of being built right into the fabric of your organization's processes and policies for worker well-being, they are nothing more than a Band-Aid, barely disguising the underlying chronic stress and dysfunction eroding your organization's ability to meet its mission. This book is about creating harmony between the individual practice of self-care and an organization's culture. Authentic self-care is a learned habit for individuals, and it needs to be embedded into organizational culture to prevent staff members from pitting their own needs against the organization's mission.

Treating self-care and well-being as an organizational *strategy* helps create a happy, healthy nonprofit, and that is what we advocate in this book. Your efforts toward self-care should be supported by your organization—something we call "WE-care." WE-care does the following:

- Recognizes self-care as an inextricable part of work.
- Acknowledges an organizational responsibility for self-care.
- Builds healthy work-life boundaries into workdays and workweeks.
- Ties passion for personal well-being to passion for organizational mission.
- Goes beyond a focus on physical health.
- Helps the nonprofit become a high-performance organization and sustain results.

As part of writing this book, we interviewed scores of nonprofit leaders, staff, and board members. What we discovered is nonprofits that practice happy, healthy ways of working are also high-performance organizations. What does that mean? According to "The Performance Imperative: A Framework for Social-Sector Excellence," from the Leap of Reason Ambassadors Community, high performance is the ability to deliver—over a prolonged period of time—meaningful, measurable, and financially sustainable results for the people or causes an organization is in existence to serve.

Says Mario Morino, chairman of the Morino Institute and cofounder of Venture Philanthropy Partners, "The Performance Imperative is a North Star guiding board, management, and staff on a journey of continuous learning and improvement. As part of the journey, a happy, healthy organization nurtures a culture that encourages curiosity, reflection, and an environment where it's safe to acknowledge challenges. Individuals in the organization are fulfilled when they see they are making a material, lasting difference for the people or causes they serve."

In an interview, Nancy Lublin, CEO of Crisis Text Line, told us "burnout is bullshit." We were taken aback. Certainly staff at a nonprofit such as Crisis Text Line, which provides counseling and intervention to people in crisis, might experience high levels of stress and burnout. But Lublin, who also founded Dress for Success and Do Something, believes that burnout equals being "out of love" with one's job, and if that's the case, she says, either that person should get another job or be asked to leave.

Lublin's zero tolerance for bad attitudes and for people who don't take care of themselves means she is willing to let people go if they aren't happy at their jobs. As a nonprofit leader, Lublin fosters an organizational culture that encourages staff to leave the office on time and have a life outside of work, builds fun into work and the workplace, and supports written and unwritten rules that prioritize self-care. Not surprisingly, Crisis Text Line is a high-performance organization.

Happy, healthy nonprofits engage their external stakeholders and deploy their skills internally to involve staff in the design and stewarding of well-being workplace initiatives. Happy, healthy nonprofits cultivate a culture of kindness, compassion, and respect as a cultural norm for how staff members work together. Author Allison Fine defines this behavior as nonprofits "working *with* rather than *at* people to create a powerful force of mutual interest," something she calls "matterness," which is also the title of her recent book on the topic.[2]

Imagine what it would it be like if all nonprofits nurtured their staffs' well-being with the same care and attention they give to external stakeholders. What if nonprofits looked internally to their staffs to get feedback and used it to continuously improve their workplace environments, cultures, and work flows? What if staff felt part of a supportive community at the office with everyone working toward the greater good, tapping into a never-ending supply of creativity and energy? If all nonprofits were happy, healthy nonprofits, think how much more effective we would be in solving some of the big social change problems of today's world.

WHY WE WROTE THIS BOOK

Writing this book together was probably inevitable given our individual interests in well-being and self-care after each of our experiences with the effects of stress and burnout. We'll talk about that in a moment, but first, a little bit of our history. We are both known for our pioneering work helping individuals, organizations, and communities leverage the power of technology and online communications for work, and we were both early adopters of the Internet and the web. In the early 1990s, Aliza blazed a path for women to embrace and benefit from technology through the company and organization she founded, Cybergrrl, Inc. and Webgrrls International. At the same time, Beth had a front row seat at the creation of a field—how nonprofits and social change activists can leverage the Internet for good, starting as a trainer and online networking evangelist for Arts Wire. We worked on nearly parallel paths over the next decade.

Then in 2013, shortly after the publication of her book, *Networked Nonprofit*, Beth lost her father, Dr. Earl Kanter, after a battle with Parkinson's disease. In the months leading up to his death, Beth criss-crossed the country on a book tour and flew home to spend time with him and tend to her own family, including two growing teens. In the process, she stopped taking care of herself.

Beth didn't notice the toll stress was taking on her until she went in for her annual physical with her doctor. Her cholesterol numbers were over 300. If you know anything about cholesterol, 150 or below is normal. Her doctor suggested that she try improving her diet, exercise, and sleep habits for six months to see if she could bring down her numbers before resorting to medications. Even walking for 30 minutes a day would help, she said.

Beth strapped on a Fitbit to get a baseline of her activity level: about 2,000 steps a day. Seeing this data forced her to evaluate how much time she spent on her rear end in front of the computer and on the phone. Beth realized she was not only sitting all day but was even using her computer keyboard as a lunch tray. Starting off with modest step goals, she added steps incrementally each week, 1,000 at a time, all the while monitoring her progress on Fitbit. She began to ask herself questions like, "What if I walked for part of my lunch hour instead of sitting? Wow, that added 2,000 steps!"

Each week, Beth upped her goal by just 1,000 steps until she got to 10,000 and beyond. Beth not only dropped 35 pounds and lowered her cholesterol, but she discovered that walking helped her manage stress and improved her ability to think clearly. She continues to walk 15,000 steps a day, gets enough sleep, and eats healthy foods as well as practices many of the techniques we outline in Chapters 4 and 5.

Aliza also experienced severe stress that began after her father's sudden and unexpected death following a botched outpatient treatment. She felt a choking feeling in her throat and tightness in her chest that led her to a cardiologist. All the tests came back normal, but she continued to experience physical symptoms that expanded to include dizziness and a pain in her gut. She finally realized that her body was exhibiting physical symptoms of stress.

Looking for relief, Aliza turned to creative practices to try to rewire her brain to respond differently to her stress and gain a sense of peace and calm. She took up painting even though she had no background in art. She only knew how good she felt when she colored or drew or dabbled in arts and crafts with her young daughter. Her instinct was that creating art would be helpful to her well-being.

Aliza bought cheap acrylic paints, paintbrushes, and canvas paper and started painting. She admits painting was really hard at first because she couldn't let go of her self-critical thinking. She found herself censoring and editing herself as she painted, trying to make things "look right." She soon realized she was using her "computer brain" when painting. She began making swirls and curlicues with her paintbrush, and started letting go of the need to make perfect art. She shifted her brain from a narrow, linear way of thinking to a more open, expansive one, immersing herself in the meditative process of putting paint on paper and reducing her stress.

Being happy and healthy isn't just something we, as authors, write about and speak about. We try to practice happy and healthy every day in our work and personal lives. This book is just one part of our combined efforts to make happy and healthy an integral part of work and life for professionals in the nonprofit sector and within the organizations where they do important work.

WHAT YOU'LL LEARN IN THIS BOOK

We've packed a lot of stories and advice from nonprofit leaders and staff in this book to help guide you and your organization along the path toward creating sustainable organizational change to avoid burnout. This book is different from typical nonprofit management books that address strategic planning, evaluation, financial matters, and all the hard skills for leading a nonprofit organization. This book gives credence to the softer skills that are the underpinning of every organization's culture and that directly affect staff members' focus and energy levels that are critical to achieving missions. We provide a practical road map for getting better results from mission-based, social change work by paying closer attention to individual and organizational well-being.

Part I of this book zeroes in on how you, as an individual, can personally move from stressed out and overwhelmed to calmer, more energized, and productive and how to bring happy, healthy practices to your workplace. Part II lays out steps toward becoming a happy, healthy nonprofit and includes examples from the field that illustrate how organizations are shifting their cultures to a greater focus on well-being with positive results.

To be sustainable, happy and healthy must align with your organization's values and be part of your organization's culture and work processes, hand-in-hand with the hard skills. We hope this book marks the start of an exciting new movement in the nonprofit sector: championing happy and healthy as essential parts of our work and workplace and everyday lives to give us the sustainable energy, focus, and fortitude we need to help make our world a better place.

How do you infuse your life, work, and organization with happy and healthy? Share your stories with us, and we will continue to chronicle them on our blogs!

Beth Kanter (bethkanter.org, @kanter)
Aliza Sherman (alizasherman.com, @alizasherman)

PART I

Revitalize Yourself

CHAPTER 1

The Problem

Why Nonprofit Professionals Burn Out

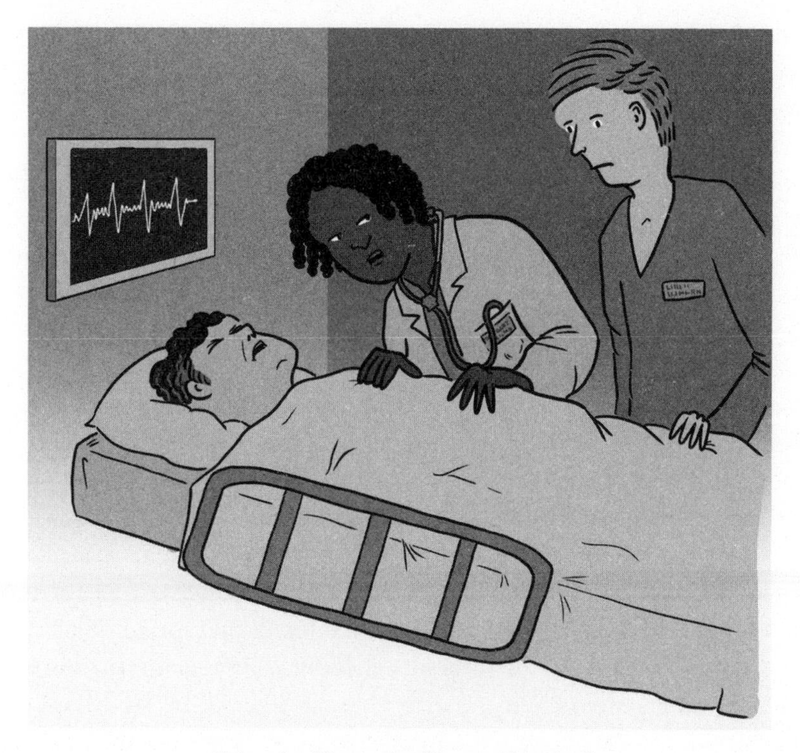

He's saying "Grant... deadline... on Thursday."

WHEN WORK AND LIFE COLLIDE

Why does something extreme have to happen before nonprofit leaders change and start to take self-care seriously?

That was the question one nonprofit executive asked after a discussion about nonprofits, self-care practices, and well-being in the workplace during the Alliance for Nonprofit Management Conference in 2015. Someone shared the story of one nonprofit leader he knew who ignored the early warning signs of burnout, kept on going, and suffered an almost-fatal heart attack. That nonprofit leader was lucky. He left the hospital in a wheelchair not a hearse. He subsequently changed his attitude and behavior, prioritizing his well-being so he could continue to lead his organization's important work.

Sacrificing one's health in service of a cause is a common narrative in the nonprofit sector. Nonprofit consultant and blogger Joan Garry[1] spent eight years as a nonprofit executive director and worked herself and her staff hard. Like most nonprofit leaders, she was so driven by her organization's mission that every task took on urgency, and there was never any downtime.

While preparing for a board meeting, Garry's development director revealed that she was wearing a heart monitor due to stress. As the organization's leader, Garry admits that she should have told her development director to go home and rest, but instead she and everyone else kept prepping for the meeting. Looking back, Garry recognizes how toxic the combination of passion for one's work and Type A behavior can be.

Garry recently told this story to an executive director who quietly confessed that one of her staff members was currently on a heart monitor. Garry asked, "What are we doing to each other? How can we take care of others when we can't take care of ourselves?"

An organization's work may be mission-based, but its people are mission critical. The passion that social change activists feel for their work is a double-edged sword. On the one hand, that fervor helps them keep going in the face of difficult challenges, especially in the early stages of their careers. On the other hand, they can be so driven they don't stop to refuel or smell the proverbial roses or even notice they are experiencing symptoms of burnout.

Aisha Moore has worked for 15 years in social justice and health care fields. One day, when leaving the office for lunch, she began to feel dizzy and light-headed. The next thing she knew, she was being wheeled out of the office on a stretcher and taken to the hospital in an ambulance. After a battery of medical tests, Moore learned from her doctor that her symptoms were the result of chronic stress.

"Stress? But I love my work," she told her doctor. Moore was so anxious at work that she did not even notice that stress was making her sick until she passed out. She recovered through a systematic program of self-care she created for herself. She then launched a wellness coaching practice to help other social changemakers avoid her mistakes.[2]

Cindy Leonard, who manages the consulting and technology programs at the Bayer Center for Nonprofit Management at Robert Morris University, was driving home from work when her heart started to race. She thought she was having a heart attack, pulled over, and dialed 911 for help. The EMTs arrived on the scene and took her vitals. They determined she was having a panic attack, not a heart attack. Leonard learned that she was experiencing an early stage of burnout due to stress. She sought help and began practicing self-care techniques to improve her well-being.[3]

Laura Maloney, currently chief operating officer at Panthera, a global conservation organization, headed up animal rescue efforts at the Louisiana Society for the Prevention of Cruelty to Animals during Hurricane Katrina. She remembers how the traumatic events affected her and her staff. Later, as the chief operating officer of The Humane Society of the United States, she oversaw the Animal Rescue Team. She noted that while staff at SPCA and The Humane Society are dedicated to their mission of saving animals from inhumane conditions, working long hours and witnessing horrible situations without any relief can be draining, even dangerous.

Maloney became a compassion fatigue educator to teach self-care practices to those in the field of animal protection who were showing early signs of burning out. Maloney recalls an exercise she facilitated at an organization where she invited staff to add ideas and suggestions to a bulletin board on self-care.

"Someone suggested that once a month, staff leave the office an hour early and do something fun as a group," she says, adding that next to the suggestion, someone else wrote, "But the animals don't leave their cages at 4 P.M. How can we take a break?"

These stories, and many more like them, illustrate how good people working in the nonprofit sector view self-care: as something that gets in the way of their work serving an important cause. Self-care is seen as a guilty pleasure, a one-time or once-in-a-while feel-good luxury instead of an individual and organizational necessity. It's time to change the status quo.

Scarcity of Self-Care

In the face of the challenging work that nonprofits tackle every day, leaders and staff need to be unapologetic about self-care. Nonprofit staff and leaders are often driven to do more with less and to keep going no matter what. But what they need to remember is by practicing self-care, they are not only taking care of themselves but also taking care of the organization's mission and all of its stakeholders.

Michelle Gislason, MA, is a senior project director at CompassPoint Nonprofit Services and well known for her leadership development and coaching work with nonprofit leaders. She often deals with leaders and organizations working to end domestic violence, work that puts nonprofit staff at risk of burnout because of potential secondary trauma. Gislason talks about radical self-care, channeling one of the leaders in the movement, Norma Wong, when she says, "We live in complex times. We need clarity of purpose and radical self-care to navigate. If our energy isn't swelling, how can we do the healing work that is needed? Lack of self-care is a form of repression. Radical self-care is an interruption of violence against ourselves."

Aspen Baker, executive director of Exhale, talks about the need for nonprofit leaders, especially those who work in social justice movements, to be more disciplined about self-care—in service of both themselves and their organizations. She points out that it is critical to distinguish between the hard work that is needed for social change and the personal sacrifices that can trigger burnout.

Baker says she learned a hard lesson by not practicing self-care in a systematic way. Instead, she and others on her staff used self-care activities as a way to escape responsibility. As a result, her organization established a nasty cycle of burnout and recovery with individuals on staff taking care of either themselves or the organization, but never both at the same time. In other words, the staff pitted their personal needs against the needs of the organization. Here's Baker's story:

> As a team, we took responsibility to redefine the meaning of "self-care." From then on, the term signified the ways in which people cared for themselves and for Exhale. The change was a choice to honor the importance of our work and to sharpen the focus required to make a lasting social impact. Now, when I think of self-care, I don't think of just manicures and massages

> or vacations and walks in the park. Self-care is not a simple feel-good activity. It's a much deeper and, ultimately, more meaningful tool. Self-care is a discipline that honors what is sacred, including the hard work that provides meaning in our lives.[4]

Baker's story demonstrates how her organization finally reframed self-care in a way that allowed staff to address personal and organizational needs simultaneously. Her story encapsulates the organizational version of self-care or "WE-care." But WE-care can't happen if all stakeholders aren't on board and engaged.

Lack of Belief, Lack of Buy-In

Nonprofit leaders, especially those who are involved in social change movements, are celebrated for giving up everything, even their health and well-being, for the cause. They work long hours, neglect their personal lives, ignore their physical and mental health, and even keep themselves from experiencing happiness and joy because of the emotionally tough work they're doing. Self-sacrifice becomes a cultural norm in organizations and movements. Leaders who give up their personal lives for the cause often evaluate staff members' value or commitment to the organization by how much they, too, deny themselves work-life separation and boundaries. These leaders perpetuate a culture that breeds a scarcity of self-care.

"I think we shouldn't be surprised by burnout in the sector," says Aria Finger, CEO at Do Something, a global organization for young people making social change. "I think it is something exacerbated by resource constraints. So when you add unbelievable passion to resource constraints, you get a situation where people are probably taking on more than they can and not caring for themselves appropriately."

What often happens to staff when carrying out the day-to-day tasks at a nonprofit—an environment with limited resources where they are often working with vulnerable clients—is that chronic stress gradually erodes their well-being, health, and relationships. In addition to an intimidating pile of work that nonprofit professionals undertake every day, there is a steady stream of clients whose lives often literally depend on the staff's efforts and the organization's programs. This kind of urgent dependency can contribute to a culture of scarcity and self-sacrifice.

"We are going to kill ourselves trying to change the world," says Brian Reich, author, strategist, and director of The Hive, a special projects unit of USA for UNHCR. "That's no good for anyone. Our work is hard, slow, messy, and stressful. We need to take care of ourselves if we expect to be successful. It's that simple."

Happy, Healthy Nonprofits are holistic entities. Your organization should examine and address stressors from all sources and set up internal programs and policies that prioritize and support self-care efforts on both individual and organizational levels. By attending to self-care in a holistic manner, your organization can go from contributing to burnout to alleviating it—or better yet, preventing it from happening in the first place.

WHAT IS BURNOUT, ANYWAY?

We keep talking about the importance of self-care for nonprofit professionals and WE-care for organizations to help reduce or prevent burnout, but what is burnout? Burnout can be defined as a state of emotional, mental, and physical exhaustion that occurs when we feel overwhelmed by too many demands, too few resources, and too little recovery time. As stress builds up, our motivation wanes. Burnout is more than just feeling tired. Burnout saps our energy, breeds negativity, reduces productivity, and can lead to feeling hopeless and even resentful.

In a blog post[5] on Idealist Careers, former Young Nonprofit Professionals Network Triangle North Carolina board member Mike Belmares shared this recipe for burnout—or what not to do—in the nonprofit sector:

- Say "yes" to everything.
- Don't have a hobby.
- Spread yourself thin.
- Do everything yourself.
- Eat, sleep, and drink your job.
- Success = staying super busy.
- Complain lots.
- Don't take vacations or personal days.
- Don't take care of yourself.
- Work only on tasks that you don't care about.

We know Belmares is being sarcastic, but he is making a powerful point. You can make good choices or bad choices in how you live and work. You can practice good habits or bad habits. Burnout doesn't happen in a day. Burnout sneaks up on you, seeping into your life little by little, making it hard to recognize and easy to ignore. If undetected and untreated, burnout can lead to an extreme situation where you are no longer able to function effectively on a personal or professional level. If you are able to read this book, you still have time to make better choices and changes in your habits and how you work to minimize your stress and avoid burnout altogether.

Kimberley MacKenzie, CFRE, a fundraising and management consultant and editor at Hilborn Charity eNEWS, recalls a time when she worked for a nonprofit where she was passionately committed despite recognizing its toxic environment. Believing in the organization's mission, she just kept working harder and harder and longer and longer, ignoring her health and personal life. Then she had a rude awakening:

> While my hair dresser was shampooing my hair one day, she told me that my hair was coming out in giant clumps and to go see a doctor. I responded, "Really?" When we have that daily stress in our lives, we can't feel what it is doing to our bodies until one day your hair is falling out, and it is too late.

In the 2014 Work Stress Survey from the American Psychological Association, 8 in 10 people reported being stressed out by work. Forty-two percent of adults surveyed also said their stress levels increased over the past five years. The stress that leads to burnout in an individual can also be contagious in a workplace culture. According to Sigal Barsade, a professor of management at the University of Pennsylvania Wharton School, "One of the things that is so insidious about [stress] being contagious is that people almost never know it is going on. When they catch the emotion from the other person, they own it, and they really think they are stressed."[6]

Catching stress or carrying it can be bad for your health and the health of your organization. Chronic stress takes a toll on our physical health, our relationships, and our overall well-being. Over time, stress can lead directly to burnout.

The Stages of Burnout

Over the past several decades, researchers have identified and articulated distinct stages of burnout. German-born American psychologist Herbert Freudenberger[7] is credited with coining the term "burnout" in 1980 and listing 12 phases of burnout including neglecting one's own needs and denial of emerging problems. In 1981, Robert L. Veninga and James P. Spradley reduced the stages to five: (1) honeymoon, (2) fuel shortage, (3) chronic symptoms, (4) crises, and (5) hitting the wall.[8] We've reworked the stages of stress based on nonprofit conditions and experiences.

The Four Steps to Nonprofit Burnout

Step 1: Passion Driven

At this early stage, you're running on a passionate belief in the cause and your organization's mission. You're ready to tackle any obstacle and believe you can get the work done. You're idealistic, energized, and hopeful.

Step 2: Passion Waning

The reality of limited resources and limiting thinking within your organization is wearing on you. You're doing the job of several people because your organization is understaffed. You wear your late nights and unpaid overtime as a badge of honor. You use sleepless nights to get done what you haven't been able to do during the day.

Step 3: Passion Challenged

You've had no relief from the stress of your work. You still believe in your organization's mission but are often too exhausted to work effectively. Your passion is in jeopardy because you have no energy to sustain it. You're making mistakes, missing deadlines, or submitting subpar work. Most likely, nobody else is noticing that you're suffering because everyone is in the same condition.

Step 4: Passion Depleted

You've lost your drive and are ready to walk away from your organization and the cause you so passionately believed in before. Every aspect of your being is suffering—your body, your mind, even your spirit. Your stress may be showing up as a short temper, anxiety and panic attacks, insomnia, or chronic illness. You don't want to admit it, but you just don't care anymore.

Not everyone gets to the last phase of burnout or even beyond that phase which is a crisis, for example, a heart attack, stroke, or mental breakdown. Some people recognize early warning signs of burnout and understand how to manage their stress and recharge their body, mind, and spirit, including using some of the techniques we describe later in this book. Which person are you?

Symptoms of Burnout

Before you think burnout comes out of nowhere, understand that burnout does give some early physical and mental warning signs even if you don't understand them or take them seriously. If you have a checklist of what to look for and can recognize it, you can do something about it before it takes its toll and moves from chronic to crisis. Psychologist Christina Maslach developed the Maslach Burnout Inventory[9] (MBI), the most widely used method of measuring burnout that examines three scales:

1. Emotional exhaustion: how overextended individuals feel from their work
2. Depersonalization: cynicism and detachment, not caring
3. Personal accomplishment: how competent and successful individuals feel in their work

Following is a breakdown of symptoms of burnout as compiled by Dr. Sherrie Bourg Carter, author of *High Octane Women: How Superachievers Can Avoid Burnout.* These telltale symptoms are some of the things Aisha Moore, Laura Maloney, Cindy Leonard, Aspen Baker, and countless other nonprofit leaders have experienced:[10]

Physical/Emotional Exhaustion	**Signs of Cynicism/Detachment**
Fatigue	Loss of enjoyment
Insomnia	Pessimism
Forgetfulness/impaired concentration and attention	Isolation
Physical symptoms	Detachment
Increased illness	**Signs of Ineffectiveness and Lack of Accomplishment**
Loss of appetite	Feelings of apathy and hopelessness
Anxiety	Increased irritability
Depression	Lack of productivity and poor performance
Anger	

The first step to avoiding burnout is to recognize when you are on the path toward it before stress-related symptoms get out of control. Do you recognize any of the symptoms above? If you do, we urge you to take those signs seriously, drop this book, and make an appointment with your doctor *right now*. In Chapter 3, we will take you through assessments so you can better identify your burnout symptoms and start making changes in your mind-set, habits, and lifestyle.

CAUSES OF BURNOUT

There are many reasons why people who work for nonprofits struggle with burnout and often experience something extreme before they change their behavior. Much has to do with strongly ingrained mind-sets that have become cultural norms in workplaces throughout the nonprofit sector that reinforce unhappy and unhealthy ways of working. Let's examine these attitudes, conditions, and trends in more detail.

Societal and Generational Attitudes

The American work ethic goes something like this: "Work long hours, and you will be rewarded." We can trace this attitude back to the Protestant work ethic, the old Calvinist idea that being a hard worker meant that you'd be preselected for Heaven. To reach "social change heaven," nonprofits need a different approach—one that prioritizes self-care as part of "doing the right thing" and not just performing a lot of tasks and perpetuating habits of continuous work without relief.

Arianna Huffington, founder of the *Huffington Post* and author of the books *Thrive* and *Sleep Revolution*, offers some insights about our culture of overwork that leads to burnout.[11] She points out that professional success and a successful life are not one and the same. Defining success in terms of your work is limited and flawed. She emphasizes that we are more than our jobs and warns us against confusing quality versus quantity of work or buying into the myth that overwork is the secret sauce for professional achievement.

"Our world is full of the casualties of this confusion," says Huffington. "Hypersuccessful people are depressed, addicted, or suffering from stress-related diseases."

From a generational standpoint, while different generations may share work values, Baby Boomers, people born between 1946 and 1964, don't share the same views of work-life balance as Generation Xers, or Gen Xers, born between 1965 and 1983. According to a 2009 report put out by Fairfield University,[12] Boomers surveyed believed that "hard work and effort would lead to success," and they were "willing to work long hours to obtain rewards." Gen Xers, however, tend to "work to live" versus "live to work" as Boomers do. They place "a lesser emphasis on work as an important part of their lives," giving rise to their nickname, "The Slacker Generation." According to a 2014 report,[13] Millennials (or Gen Y) "strive for work-life balance, but this tends to mean 'work-me balance,' not 'work-family balance.' They want time for themselves and space for their own self-expression."

Maddie Grant, coauthor of *When Millennials Take Over: Preparing for the Ridiculously Optimistic Future of Business*, discovered through research for her book that Millennials are initially attracted to working at nonprofits because of the organization's values and mission. However, they care deeply about work-life balance. Grant says Millennials look at a work-life balance spectrum—education, work, and fun in the space of one day—compared to older generations that spread out their lives in terms of education, work, retire, then have fun. Grant says this means that Millennials want well-being baked into the workplace to support the way they practice work-life balance, and if it is missing, they will work elsewhere.

According to a report by the Young Nonprofit Professionals Network (YNPN), *Stepping Up or Stepping Out: A Report on the Readiness of Next Generation Nonprofit Leaders*, more than 90 percent of leaders surveyed reported burnout as the main reason for leaving the sector and 69 percent pointed to job-related stress. These young leaders are not enthusiastic about taking on the role of executive director in a nonprofit organization, expressing concerns because of the high levels of stress and long hours.

As one young leader interviewed for the study said, "It's very important for me to be able to have a happy, healthy, and fulfilling personal life in addition to my career. The climate I have observed in many nonprofits does not support this. [There is an expectation] that leaders, especially EDs, will take on challenging, stressful schedules with relatively low pay because they believe in 'the cause.'"

Nonprofit Sector Mind-Sets

We've touched on some societal and generational mind-sets regarding work, success, and work-life balance, all of which can factor in to why one nonprofit professional might burn out and another might not. Regardless of one's generation, there are mind-sets that could affect them that are firmly entrenched in the nonprofit sector in general. The following are a few of them.

The Nonprofit Starvation Cycle

One common nonprofit mind-set is the "Nonprofit Starvation Cycle"[14] that makes nonprofits so hungry for adequate infrastructure that they can barely function as organizations—let alone serve others or deliver programs. The vicious cycle begins with funders' unrealistic expectations about how much money running a nonprofit takes and results in nonprofits misrepresenting their costs while skimping on vital systems.

Many nonprofits look at workplace wellness and well-being programs from a lens of doing without. Says Mark Horvath, founder of Invisible People, who worked on the frontlines at a homeless shelter in Los Angeles:

> The tech start-up community has learned that employee benefits such as gym memberships or being allowed free time to work on your own projects help increase employee productivity and wellness. There is zero funding for employee wellness in the nonprofit sector. Funders could change that by adding a percentage of grants that have to go to making workplace environments better and thus increasing the outcomes of their grant funding. Nonprofits have to rely on unrestricted funds to do anything for employees. Those funds are precious and used for the gaps restricted funding doesn't cover.

Clayton Lord, vice president of Local Arts Advancement at Americans for the Arts, says that low wages and high workloads combined with personal passion and strong belief in the mission create the perfect storm to burn people out. He calls this an "alternative currency of personal passion."

"This sets up a bad dynamic when it comes to self-care. At best, it means that staff aren't asking for the conditions and compensation they deserve, and at worst, it morphs into a sort of martyrdom in which we compensate for our lack of money, time, support, and work-life balance by working so hard for so little," says Lord.

Many nonprofits settle into a "low pay, make do, and do without"[15] culture, according to the *Nonprofit Overhead Cost Study*. Every aspect of an organization feels the pinch of this culture that manifests in a number of ways including personal financial strain, not enough staff or systems in place, and lack of investment in professional and leadership development. Self-care measures are not even considered for implementation because they are perceived as unaffordable luxuries. A culture dominated by "do without" thinking accelerates staff burnout, and the cycle continues.

Funder-Driven Stress

According to an article in *The Foundation Review* titled "Talent Philanthropy: Investing in Nonprofit People to Advance Nonprofit Performance," the lack of foundation funding for nonprofit talent infrastructure results in the social sector suffering from "poor recruitment, retention, and retirement, which could in turn be causing serious damage to performance and sustainability."[16] Ira Hirschfield, president of the Evelyn & Walter Haas Jr. Fund, puts it this way:

> Foundations ask a great deal of the organizations we support—to strengthen community, meet urgent needs for services, solve complex environmental problems, influence public policy, and build and sustain movements for change. . . . So it's striking how seldom we back that up with funds to help organizations develop and strengthen the ability of their leaders to meet those high expectations.[17]

Marissa M. Tirona, director of Blue Shield Against Violence, leads the foundation's programmatic and grant-making efforts to address, prevent, and ultimately end domestic violence. She observed that when a nonprofit and its leader do not have a total clarity of purpose, they are unable to say no to funding that is outside of the scope of their mission and lack the ability to implement. This creates unmanageable workloads on top of already stressful work that leads to overworking and helps perpetuate the scarcity of self-care. Says Tirona, "Organizations need to operate from a position of strength."[18]

At the highest level, funders can be catalysts for positive change by recognizing, acknowledging, and addressing problems that create unnecessary organizational stress. They can also identify stress factors in the sector which, left unchecked, could wreak havoc on organizations and social change movements. Funders can actively resource solutions to address problems before they lead to burnout. While funders should not be the only group identifying problems that should be addressed within the sector or within organizations, they are often the only ones with sufficient resources to put toward solving problems that are identified.

Scarcity Mind-Set

The scarcity mind-set is related to the Nonprofit Starvation Cycle. A scarcity mind-set is defined as the belief that everything is limited. The scarcity assumption is based on the thinking that *there's not enough of what our nonprofit needs to go around,* and *there's more out there that our organization needs, but we don't have it.*

Here is how the scarcity mind-set plays out in many nonprofit organizations and demotes the pressing need for self-care:

> *There's not enough time to get everything done with limited staff, so staff needs to work long hours and sacrifice self-care to get results.*

When we function under a scarcity mind-set, we perceive, manage, and deal with problems differently and often poorly. Using self-care techniques, mindfulness practices, and attention to organizational well-being, you can shift thinking from scarcity to abundance.

Myth of Being Indispensable

In the study, "The Voices of Nonprofit Talent," nonprofit employees were characterized as being "known for their dedication to their jobs, devotion to their organization's missions, and passion for their careers."[19] According to the study, 84 percent of jobseekers didn't look at nonprofit work as solely a way to make a living but as a part of their identities. Social change activists can be committed to their work with such intensity, but this absorption by one's job can stand in the way of practicing self-care and result in burnout.

The correlation between work and one's identity without boundaries is what Vu Le, executive director of Rainier Valley Corps and author of the *Nonprofit with Balls* blog, calls "The Myth of Indispensability." Le suggests that nonprofit workers are so busy dealing with pressing work, where often lives literally depend on what they do, that they begin to feel indispensable and that their organization will collapse if they are not working long hours with no time off. When nonprofit professionals buy into that myth, their personal lives and well-being suffers.

Le relates a story on his blog about a colleague and mentor of his who called him for some advice:

> Her mother was showing signs of health problems. "Should I take a break from work and move down to take care of her?" she asked. I thought of the importance of my friend's work and her integrity in always getting things done. And then I thought of my mother and the things I wish I had done, the words I could have said, the time I could have spent.

Le said that the very fact his friend had to think twice about choosing between work and family was a sign of attitudes in the nonprofit sector and the dedication of nonprofit professionals. Not all types of dedication are healthy.

Lack of Leadership Development

In 2013, the Meyer Foundation[20] surveyed nearly 100 executive directors of nonprofit organizations to learn how it could best support them. Executive directors mentioned challenges that affected their effectiveness including when working with boards, fundraising, and managing personnel. The survey showed that most executive directors saw strong links between their professional leadership development opportunities as well as personal well-being (physical and mental health, and work-life balance) and organizational effectiveness.

The nonprofit sector has historically underinvested in leadership development. According to a report from Foundation Center, the nonprofit sector spent $400 million on leadership development in 2011, but that translated to only 0.03 percent of the sector's $1.5 trillion total annual spending. To drill down further, the nonprofit sector spent $29 per person on leadership development compared with $120 in the private sector. Foundation funding was also a factor, with only 1 percent going each year to leadership development initiatives for their grantee organizations over a 20-year period.[21]

The report also quotes a 2013 study, "Shaping the Future," stating that 32 percent of nonprofit leaders identified balancing personal life and work as a skill they needed to develop. While nonprofits may have work-life policies in place such as comp time, those policies are not being implemented. The report suggests that nonprofit boards should hire "people-focused leaders" and establish "guiding principles and policies for a supportive work environment."

Many nonprofit leaders sacrifice so much of their personal lives and make themselves sick in service of their communities. Nonprofit leaders often give up quality time with their families and friends, avoid the relief of downtime, and neglect their professional and personal development. Organizations need to implement leadership development programs that educate, encourage, and fund their leaders to incorporate self-care and mindfulness techniques for themselves so they can model happier and healthier behavior to their staff. Leaders should be rewarded with sabbaticals before they burn out, not as crisis triage after burnout occurs.

Developing more people-focused leaders can help transform toxic nonprofit cultures and greatly reduce organization-wide passion fatigue and burnout. When nonprofit leaders take time for leadership development and sabbatical programs to replenish their own energy, they come back refreshed and that benefits the organization.[22]

THE STRESS OF WORK

There are many reasons why stress can stem from your work. In an article on the Mayo Clinic website titled "Job Burnout: How to Spot It and Take Action," a number of factors that lead to job burnout were listed, any of which could adversely affect your health and well-being:

- Lack of control
- Unclear job expectations
- Dysfunctional workplace dynamics
- Mismatch in values
- Poor job fit
- Extremes of activity
- Lack of social support
- Work-life imbalance

According to the American Psychological Association (APA) report, *Stress in the Workplace*, a survey of 1,546 working adults found that 44 percent felt their stress levels have increased over the past five years.[23] More than a third said they felt tense or stressed out during their workday. Many cited low salaries, lack of opportunities for advancement, heavy workloads, unrealistic job expectations, and long hours as factors that increased stress.

Stressful Overwork

Long hours at work have been directly tied to health problems in workers. Researchers quoted in the article "The Impact of Overtime and Long Work Hours on Occupational Injuries and Illnesses," published in *Occupational and Environment Medicine* stated, "studies have associated overtime and extended work schedules with an increased risk of hypertension, cardiovascular disease, fatigue, stress, depression, musculoskeletal disorders, chronic infections, diabetes, general health complaints," leading to death.[24] Believe it or not, Japan has a term for the effects of this type of work: *karōshi* or "death by overwork." If that isn't a reason not to work overtime and long hours, we don't know what is!

Research about working long hours suggests overwork does not help us be more productive. In a study of consultants by Erin Reid, a professor at Boston University's Questrom School of Business, managers could not tell the difference between employees who actually worked 80 hours a week and those who pretended to.[25] Reid did not find that the employees who pretended to work accomplished less or that the overworking employees accomplished more. In fact, establishing required time off for employees can increase a team's productivity.

Josh Bennett, growth manager at ActionSprout, worked at a large corporation on an internal study of employee burnout doing interviews and running surveys and then slicing data. According to Bennett, burnout occurs when an employee or volunteer has reached the limit of his or her physical and/or emotional strength. Often people associate this with stress and long hours, tight deadlines, and so on, but such things are often symptoms of a deeper organizational dysfunction.

"It is easy to focus on these problems and overlook the role of the manager or supervisor on the atmosphere, clarity of expectations and organization of workflows, and respect for personal time and space.

Inexperienced management and unclear expectations are often the most damaging. As it turns out, the two are not mutually exclusive, and in many cases, one begets the other," says Bennett. With respect to personal time and space, employees or volunteers are often more than happy to work the long hours for and with people they trust, says Bennett.

"Trust is a completely different discussion that touches on transparency, team dynamics, and so much more. The manager and organization need to be aware of the physical and emotional state of the team and when the employee or volunteer has gone home or is on vacation, or even just stepping out of the office for a walk, they must be left alone—barring any emergencies. The manager and the team should ask themselves, before picking up the phone or texting the person, 'Can it wait?' More often than not, it can," Bennett explains.

Bennett warns against managers seeing employees or volunteers as tools or as a means to an end rather than as people. Managers should focus on the progress made and things learned rather than strictly on the results of the task. Even though the bottom line for nonprofits is their mission and not their financial performance, overwork does affect an organization's budget with higher health insurance costs and higher employee turnover.[26] As we mentioned before, research shows that when staff members log long hours, specifically more than 40 hours a week, it actually costs the organization more because they are less productive.[27] With all of this evidence of the negative results of working long hours, it doesn't make any sense that any organization still allows—even encourages, rewards, or at the very least turns a blind eye to—staff who put in long hours.

Stressful Work

The way nonprofit professionals work or overwork can cause stress, but in some cases, stress can manifest in an organization due to the nature of the work itself. When left unchecked, these unavoidable stressors can result in compassion fatigue or secondary traumatic stress (STS). SaraKay Smullens defines compassion fatigue in her book, *Burnout and Self-Care in Social Work,* as "the overall experience of emotional and physical fatigue that social service professionals experience due to chronic use of empathy when working with clients who are suffering in some way."

STS is common among nurses and urgent care professionals, relief workers in war-torn regions, and workers dealing with other emotionally charged situations such as the Syrian Refugee crisis. In 2016, the United Nations High Commissioner for Refugees (UNHCR) released "Staff Well-Being and Mental Health in UNHCR Survey,"[28] the first-ever comprehensive research on the UNHCR staff's mental health. The survey found that the risk for secondary traumatic stress was identified in 38 percent of the respondents who worked directly with clients.

The symptoms of STS or compassion fatigue are similar to the burnout symptoms we discussed earlier. Invisible People's Horvath[29] shared this story:

> While temping at a shelter front desk answering phones one day, I was getting emotionally burnt saying "no" far more than I was saying "yes." I remember turning away a mother with five children. It messed me up and got me thinking about the emotional stress frontline workers go through on a daily basis.

When you compound stressful work with bad habits like sleep deprivation, no exercise, poor nutrition, toxic relationships, and the inability to set boundaries, you create a recipe for something to go terribly wrong. Even when you can't change the nature of stressful work, you can strengthen yourself to resist compassion fatigue and other more serious physical and mental effects of stress and burnout.

Physical Work Environments

Walk into any nonprofit workplace and what do you see? Like most office settings, you see desks and chairs—lots of chairs. You can practically feel the malaise and energy drain when you are in an office filled with people sitting—sitting at their desks all day long, sitting in meetings in the conference room, sitting on their breaks. In most offices, people sit more than they stand, stretch, or walk. Scientists in Australia published an article in the *British Journal of Sports Medicine* that stated, on average, people sit for 9.3 hours a day compared to 7.7 hours a day of sleeping.[30]

Dr. James A. Levine, obesity researcher at the Mayo Clinic and author of the book *Get Up: Why Your Chair Is Killing You and What You Can Do About It*, explains that our bodies were not designed for sitting, but over the past 200 years, there has been a slow and insidious shift in our workplaces. The Industrial Revolution of the early 1800s led to building of factories followed by the Second Industrial or Technological Revolution that led to the ability to construct office buildings to accommodate the growing population of office workers. The office chair—a public health enemy—became a staple of the office environment and began to contribute to a more sedentary culture. Sitting became an indicator of productivity in an office. If you were not sitting at your desk all day long, you were not working. Walking around equaled goofing off.

Sitting is now so embedded in our work-obsessed culture that we don't even question why we do it. And, because everyone in the office is doing it, we experience a subtle peer pressure to sit still. As Nilofer Merchant points out in her popular Ted Talk, "sitting is the smoking of our generation."[31]

Scientific and medical communities agree that there are serious health risks to a sedentary work style. If you are sitting throughout the day, you are not burning calories. Obesity can be the consequence and that can lead to diabetes, high cholesterol, swollen ankles, and many other physical problems. The health burden of sitting also affects your mind. Sitting makes you "stale," according to Levine, and that can have a direct impact on your desire to do good things in the world. Levine invented the treadmill desk to try to address the issue of sitting too much. Later in this book, we will share tips and stories from nonprofits that have busted the culture of sitting and made movement a part of work and integrated self-care.

Technology Ubiquity

Our "always on" digital lifestyle challenges our ability to find solitude or to contemplate quietly. We have all become such experts at being hyperconnected, always in touch and informed, that we have forgotten how to embrace time away from digital devices, screens, and electronic communications. This lack of stillness time can accelerate the symptoms of burnout. We need to practice self-care around our use of technology and strive for tech wellness.

You know the scenario. A nonprofit executive director sends out an e-mail during the weekend to staff asking for a work task to be done, and the expectation is that the staff will not only check their e-mail over the weekend but also do the work. Or perhaps a nonprofit staff person is on vacation but still checks work e-mail or social media. Mobile devices provide us with instant connection and constant distraction. Our continuous use of these devices blurs the line between work and downtime.

While technology is not completely to blame for burning us out, the fact that we are so readily connected to our work through our mobile devices can lead to the overworking we've already described. Stewart Friedman, Wharton practice professor of management and director of the Wharton Work/Life Integration Project, says, "If you look at the span of the last 50 years, we know people are working more, that more of their waking attention is devoted to work and work-related decisions, and it's a challenge because the ubiquity of technology has enabled 24/7 communication."[32] Friedman goes on to say that most of us didn't grow up with the tech tools of today. We haven't established boundaries between work and other parts of our lives caused by this new connectivity. Monitoring and controlling the impacts of using our connected devices on our lives are new skills we need to acquire.

Pew Research Center conducted a survey on mobile device usage in 2015.[33] The report actually stated that people "often treat [their mobile devices] like body appendages." Ninety-four percent of smartphone owners said they carry their phone with them frequently, and 82 percent said they never or rarely turn their phones off. Having a mobile phone in your pocket during your downtime makes checking or reading work e-mail only one tap away, a distracting temptation during your time away from work.

Brandon T. McDaniel, a doctoral candidate in human development and family studies at Penn State, coined the term *technoference*[34] to express the interference from technology on couples' relationships. We believe technoference is present in all of our interactions with others, whether the person we're with is half-listening to us during a conversation because of a smartphone notification or we're the ones stealing a peek at our own devices.

Being able to unplug and disconnect can lead to improved relationships with others as well as less physical and emotional stress, better sleep, increased focus and memory, and increased workplace productivity. Digital health both in the workplace and at home is integral to self-care activities, but often tech wellness is left out of wellness and well-being conversations and programs. We cover tech wellness practices later in this book.

Information Overload

We often hear complaints from nonprofit professionals about being "content fried."[35] We all have so much content in our professional lives, and it comes rushing at us from our e-mail inboxes and social networks through our mobile devices, compounding the deluge of work-related information we already get through paper and snail mail. We scan, we browse, and we try to thoughtfully read the best information and carry out online conversations all day long and into the night.

Having to process so much information on a daily basis can lead to difficulty concentrating, shortened attention spans, or feeling overwhelmed, all symptoms of burnout. "Attention span" is the amount of time we concentrate on a task without becoming distracted. Most educators and psychologists agree that the ability to focus attention on a task is crucial for the achievement of one's goals. According to the Statistic Brain website's list of attention span statistics, in 2000, humans had a 12-second attention span; in 2013, it was down to 8 seconds.[36] To put our attention span deficit into context, a goldfish has an attention span of 9 seconds! It's no surprise our attention spans have been decreasing over the past decade with the increase of social media, mobile phones, and the flood of online information.

The common act of checking your e-mail has a physical affect on your body, creating a flight or fight response—what writer Linda Stone calls "e-mail apnea." Next time you check your e-mail—and don't do that before you finish reading this chapter—notice if you are intermittently holding your breath. You may be depriving your body and brain of a steady stream of oxygen and putting yourself on a roller coaster of physiological changes resulting in stress.

Stone also came up with the term *continuous partial attention*[37], or CPA, to explain the process of trying to pay attention to a number of sources of incoming information at the same time but at a superficial level. If you are toggling in short bursts between trying to accomplish a task that requires concentration and checking your e-mail or social networks, you are doing yourself and your organization a disservice.

Training your attention and engaging in more mindful consumption of information online are essential nonprofit self-care skills. Later in this book, we tell you how to use brain science to reduce information overload as well as share mindfulness techniques to help you develop better focus habits and avoid being like a goldfish with ADHD!

MOVING OUT OF BURNOUT

Contrary to a lot of things we've shared with you in this chapter, your situation is not all doom and gloom. You can positively affect your work and life when you make a conscious commitment to, and form an intentional practice of, self-care. Your goal is not to simply start scheduling isolated activities for yourself like taking a spa day or getting a massage. Your goal should be to make happy and healthy an overall framework for your life and work. Your self-care must be inseparable from your personal passion for social change as well as be an integral part of your organization's strategy and values.

Are you ready to move from a chronic state of stress to a chronic state of self-care? Are you ready to become happy and healthy? Read on!

CHAPTER 2

The Foundation

Understanding the Areas of Self-Care

Well, on the up-side, I'm a shoo-in to win the office sleep-deprivation pool.

DEALING WITH STRESS

Now that we've covered the problem of burnout in the nonprofit sector and what can cause it, we'll lay out the areas in your life where you could have stress. Sometimes, chronic stress becomes so much a part of your life that you don't recognize it or the toll it is taking on you until burnout occurs. Chronic stress can wear you down and make you sick and unhappy.

A major step to avoiding the damage your stress can cause all around you is to take care of yourself first. A common analogy that highlights the importance of prioritizing self-care is the instruction you hear from flight attendants when you travel:

Put your oxygen mask on first, then help others.

Translation: You're no good to anyone—not your family, not your friends or community, not even your employer, coworkers, or the people you want to serve—if you are depleted of energy and unable to function at your optimal levels. Recognizing your stress symptoms and triggers is important. Even more critical is to know whether you are dealing with your stress using negative behaviors or positive self-care routines. Self-care can be a powerful way to reduce your stress.

WHAT IS SELF-CARE, REALLY?

Self-care is about revitalization. Self-care requires that you take a more holistic view of who you are and *how* you are, from head to toe, inside and out, to gauge where you're lacking and where you're full. You are more than your resume and work, more than your passions and mission. You bring far more to your organization than simply your knowledge, skills, and abilities. You need to acknowledge and honor all aspects of yourself—physical, mental, emotional, and spiritual—and understand how ignoring yourself and failing to care for yourself opens the door to dysfunction and disease within you and within your organization. Self-care gives you the sustainable energy you need to do your mission-driven work.

But take heed! According to *Nonprofit with Balls* blogger Vu Le, self-care can be abused. Nonprofit staff using self-care as a work avoidance strategy places more stress on coworkers and affects those individuals' career advancement opportunities, perhaps even getting them labeled as "slackers." Le says, "Maybe because burnout is a serious problem in our sector, some nonprofit staff, especially the newer professionals, are trying hard to inoculate themselves from that happening to them."

Self-care should not be used as an excuse to avoid work, but Le says he's witnessed it. "In some ways, maybe because we talk so much about it, self-care has become somewhat of a punch line to various jokes: 'Hey, are you attending that breakfast gala of one of our partner organizations?' 'Nope! Self-care!'"

Treat self-care as part of work and part of doing better work. When Aisha Moore, who we introduced in Chapter 1, realized she was burned out, part of her revitalization started with creating a Bill of Rights around self-care so she would not feel guilty about prioritizing taking care of herself. Your first step on the road toward revitalization is to declare your own Self-Care Bill of Rights. Here is Moore's:

Self-Care Bill of Rights[1]

I have the right to:

- Put my mental, physical, emotional, and spiritual health above everything and everyone else.
- Put self-love into action.
- Give to others and this world in a way that energizes me.
- Make decisions about my time without guilt.
- Adequate sleep.
- Focus on my physical body and outward appearance.
- Pamper myself.
- Define leadership and success in a way that supports self-love in action.
- Develop new habits that support my self-care.
- Speak the truth in all situations.

Self-care can directly affect your levels of happiness and health through attention, awareness, and attendance.

- *Attention* to you, the individual, as an integral part of the whole organization.
- *Awareness* of issues or situations that are causing problems for you.
- *Attendance* to the root of the problems that are adversely affecting you.

Self-care isn't about a quick fix from a meditation session, a massage, or an unplugged weekend—but any or all of those things can be incorporated into our lives, adopted as new habits, and become as essential to our day as brushing our teeth or bathing. Individual self-care can result in a boost in organizational productivity because the happier, healthier individual can relate better to others, cope better with stress, and experience more sustainable energy to apply to the work and mission. Bottom line: your self-care practices are good for your organization!

Self-care involves taking deliberate and consistent steps to prioritize your physical, mental, and emotional health. According to the University of Buffalo School of Social Work Self-Care Starter Kit,[2] reducing work-related stress is not enough. Self-care is about enhancing your overall well-being, at work, at home, and everywhere else you interact.

INTRODUCING THE FIVE SPHERES OF HAPPY HEALTHY LIVING

As a human being, you are affected by and influenced by your relationships, both internal and external. How you relate with yourself, with others, and with your surroundings and other elements can have a direct impact on your well-being. There are some fundamental areas of your life that deserve your attention. You can experience stress in each of these areas, and you can also apply self-care techniques in each area to better attend to your well-being and manage your stress levels. We call these areas the Five Spheres of Happy Healthy Living.

The Five Spheres of Happy Healthy Living make up how you exist in the world. These areas intersect as you live your life and directly affect how well you exist and work on a daily basis. When there is well-being in these areas, you live with more ease. When any of these areas are unbalanced or infected with internal or external stressors, you can fall into dis-ease—literally sickness, critical illness, and even early death. Remember Aisha Moore's story: She didn't recognize that the dire physical symptoms she was experiencing were caused by stress. When any of the spheres of your life are out of sync and you experience stress, you can infect others.

Here's a quick overview of the Five Spheres of Happy Healthy Living, the areas of your life that define how you relate and interact in your world.

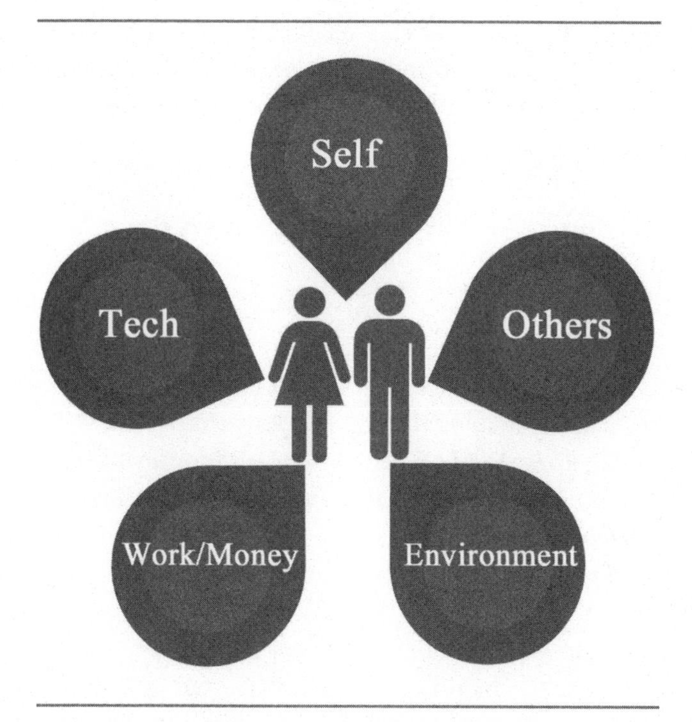

- Sphere 1: Self. How you take care of yourself—mentally, physically, and spiritually. Without prioritizing self-care, all other spheres suffer or fall apart.
- Sphere 2: Others. This can include family, friends, acquaintances and strangers, and people in your communities, including online communities. Your relationships with your coworkers can fit in here but also in Sphere 4. You can't avoid how your interactions with others—good and bad—affect your entire self.
- Sphere 3: Environment. Indoor and outdoor environments are a major force in your life, but you may move through spaces and places with little awareness of their impact.
- Sphere 4: Work and Money. When you don't have good boundaries and emotions around work or money, it can create tension and deep, underlying stress.
- Sphere 5: Tech. Your continuous access to personal technology and the Internet through your mobile device adds this new sphere to your life. Your relationship to your tech can negatively affect your well-being, and there are finally longer-term studies to prove this.

Let's dig more deeply into the Five Spheres of Happy Healthy Living to better understand how everything in your life is interconnected and how making small, deliberate changes through self-care can generate huge, positive results.

SPHERE 1: RELATIONSHIP TO SELF

Knowing yourself and taking care of yourself on a daily basis with deliberate intention helps you approach your work in a more refreshed, energized, and focused manner. To better examine how to approach self-care, we start by looking through the lens of a Wellness Triad, three aspects of living that make up the foundation for enhanced well-being: sleep, nutrition, and exercise. These three areas are intricately interconnected. Developing better sleep, eating, and fitness habits helps your body and brain resist the negative effects of stress that you inevitably face during your day.

Managing stress through proper sleep, nutrition, and exercise can set you up for a renewed ability to perform at your best in all aspects of life and work. Your nonprofit's health care benefits may include wellness screenings or health coaching. Utilize these resources to help assess what changes you need to make. Seek advice from your doctor or other medical professional before changing your sleep, eating, and exercise habits, especially if you have any preexisting health issues.

Start with a Good Night's Sleep

With so much on your plate, where can you start to make a noticeable change in the way you live and work? Start with sleep. According to the Centers for Disease Control and Prevention (CDC), insufficient sleep is a "public health problem."[3] Blogger Maria Popova, of the popular culture blog *Brain Pickings*, sums up the connection between sleep and self-care in this quote:

> We tend to wear our ability to get by on little sleep as some sort of badge of honor that validates our work ethic. But what it really is is a profound failure of self-respect and of priorities.[4]

As Arianna Huffington, who wrote *Sleep Revolution*, says, "Sleep is a fundamental human need that must be respected."[5] Huffington learned the hard way about respecting sleep, passing out in her office from sleep deprivation and waking up in a pool of blood with a broken cheekbone and cut over her eye. Her experience should tell you that sleeplessness is not a necessary sacrifice to prove your devotion to your organization's mission.

Be honest: How much sleep do you get each night? Are you sleeping through the night? Do you wake up feeling refreshed? If not, you need to address the issue of insufficient sleep to make a foundational shift in your overall well-being. Greg McKeown, author of *Essentialism: The Disciplined Pursuit of Less*, devotes an entire chapter of his book to the importance of protecting sleep. If, as McKeown says, our best asset for changing the world is ourselves, then we need to invest in, and not damage, our greatest asset.

How much sleep does your body actually need? Is there a magic number? The amount of hours per night varies from person to person and is different based on age. The National Sleep Foundation, a champion of sleep science and sleep health for individuals, undertook a comprehensive research study to answer the question of sufficient sleep and provides evidence-based guidelines on how much sleep you really need at each age.[6] Drumroll, please . . . adults need between seven and nine hours of sleep per night.

You may have already learned the hard way, like Huffington, what cheating yourself out of a good night's sleep can do to your well-being. But are you doing anything about it?

"I realized that there was a disconnect between what I knew helped me be at my best and most productive, and what I was actually doing in practice," admits nonprofit consultant Joyce Lee-Ibarra, who was not enforcing good sleeping habits for herself. Some simple changes Lee-Ibarra made are outlined in Chapter 4.

So what's the bottom line about sleep? Ignoring your body and brain's need for quality sleep is destructive, and you'll pay for it with decreased mental capacity, increased stress and anxiety, and a weakened ability to perform complex tasks and even basic ones. A lack of sleep will make it harder for you to make small changes in your habits to avoid stress and incorporate self-care activities. To address your sleep issues, try monitoring and tracking the number of hours you're getting per night and how you feel, then start to shift your sleep routine to a healthier habit.

You Really Are What You Eat

What we eat and drink can affect how our bodies and brains work and even how well we sleep. Vice versa, a well-rested body and brain can process the foods we eat more efficiently. Knowing what we put into our bodies can mean the difference between being strong, clear-headed, and effective or being sluggish, dull, and slow. Two steps to enhancing our well-being through nutrition are learning about the best foods for our health and changing our eating habits to ensure we consume them. Understanding what we should not consume and developing the willpower to avoid what is bad for us is just as important.

The Stress Management Society in the United Kingdom[7] lays out some very straightforward tips for proper nutrition such as:

1. Avoid fast food.
2. Don't skip meals.
3. Limit caffeine intake.
4. Avoid sugary and fatty foods.
5. Don't go on fad diets.
6. Don't pick at your food.

Simple, right? Enough of the "don'ts." The Stress Management Society also provides some "do's" such as fortifying your body with vitamins A (supports vision), B (supports your nervous system), and C (protects immune system and reduces cortisol levels); proteins (tissue repair); and magnesium (muscle relaxation, fatty acid formation, new cell production, and heartbeat regulation) to combat stress. Seek the guidance of your doctor if you plan on making changes to your diet, especially if you have any underlying health conditions.

Get a Move on It

In a 2015 article in the *Annals of Internal Medicine* titled "Sedentary Time and Its Association with Risk for Disease Incidence, Mortality, and Hospitalization in Adults," our sedentary lifestyle is identified as a major factor for illness and disease.[8] Many of us spend half of our waking hours sitting, and our inactivity could be the early death of us. If that isn't a wake-up call, we don't know what is! We all need to once and for all shift away from looking at exercise as a chore and incorporate more movement into our lives as part of our daily routines and as part of our work.

Studies show that exercise can relieve stress, reduce depression, and improve cognitive function, according to the Anxiety and Depression Association of America.[9] But even if you intellectually understand the benefits of managing your stress and how fitness can play an important roll in reducing stress, you may not be finding the wherewithal to stick to a regular fitness routine to make real strides in improving your health and well-being. In the 2014 *Stress in America* report from the American Psychological Association, Americans surveyed continued to "report stress at levels higher than what they believe is healthy, struggle to achieve their health and lifestyle goals, and manage stress in ineffective ways."[10]

How much exercise and at what intensity will help us live a healthier, longer life? The Department of Health and Human Services[11] recommends doing one of the following each week for moderate health benefits:

- 150 minutes (2 hours and 30 minutes) of moderate-intensity aerobic physical activity (such as brisk walking or tennis)
- 75 minutes (1 hour and 15 minutes) each week of vigorous-intensity aerobic physical activity (such as jogging or swimming laps)
- An equivalent combination of moderate- and vigorous-intensity aerobic physical activity

Looking at these numbers can feel daunting. Integrating movement into your life is not always an easy habit to get started or maintain, but the results can be significant. According to a wellness blog post in the *New York Times*, people who followed the guidelines above literally—doing 150 minutes per week of moderate exercise—were at 31 percent less risk of dying during the 14-year study period compared to nonexercisers. The overachievers who worked out moderately, mostly walking, for 450 minutes per week or a little more than one hour per day were 39 percent less likely to die prematurely. We'll take those numbers!

You don't need to be an overachiever or an Olympic athlete to reap some benefits from exercise. The point is to start with the first step. Even a 30-minute daily brisk walk can do wonders for feeling good.

Down Time

People in the nonprofit sector often feel a strong sense of service to the cause or their clients. This kind of passion and devotion can come at the expense of their personal downtime, resulting in working on weekends, not taking vacation days, or canceling on activities with friends or family. Sound familiar? While self-sacrifice might seem noble or be culturally engrained in your organization, the truth is you can't sustain your passion if you do not take some time off or away to do something other than work. Repeat after us: "I am not just my work."

Aisha Moore says when she didn't have a self-care plan, she woke up 20 minutes before she had to leave for work, leaving no time for herself at the start of the day. "I gave everything to my job. As part of my self-care plan, I incorporate downtime, which involves a mindfulness activity—whether adult coloring, journaling, meditation, tidying my house, or whatever. I've created a Saturday morning feeling before I start my workday." Moore says this time allows her to have more energy and be more productive at her job.

"If our whole life is our work, with no outside hobbies or downtime, we have very little left for ourselves at the end of the day," says Moore.

"Prioritize personal time and vacation, and encourage your coworkers to do the same," says Amanda Evrard, development director at NOWCastSA. Says Evrard, "All staff need to feel comfortable with taking vacation days, as opposed to believing that their absence is only seen as a burden on everyone else left behind. And in the event that your organization doesn't value personal time, or specific coworkers aren't taking time away, advocate for others and ensure they aren't being overworked for the collective good."

The Wellness Triad and having down time are some critical pieces to caring for your Sphere of Self, but you don't exist in a vacuum. Honoring vacation time and respecting communication boundaries are important aspects of workplace well-being that we will discuss later. Let's move on to caring for the next sphere.

SPHERE 2: RELATIONSHIP TO OTHERS

If you are experiencing optimal levels of well-being, it stands to reason that your happy, healthy state can have a positive affect on the well-being of the people around you, such as your family and friends as well as your coworkers and organization as a whole. Conversely, if you are stressed out, depleted, frustrated, and burned out, you can directly affect the well-being of those around you in negative ways.

The 2011 *Canadian Work, Stress, and Health Study* showed that "work contact was associated with higher levels of work-to-family conflict, distress and sleep problems."[12] Simply put, phone calls and e-mails after work hours invade your personal life and interfere with your ability to decompress, increasing your stress.

Says Nancy Smyth, dean of the University of Buffalo School of Social Work, "I do not check my work e-mail on the weekend and never on vacation. This keeps me from obsessing about a contentious e-mail through the weekend that would end up making the time off very stressful. Staff know to text or call me if there is truly something urgent that I need to see."

Family, Friends, Community

When stressed out, you often end up taking out your frustrations on those closest to you, reserving your small pockets of patience for work because you might worry more about getting reprimanded or fired than you do about being kicked out of your home. You know you shouldn't do it, but when you're at the end of your rope, you have fewer coping mechanisms and end up turning your home into a slow cooker of leftover cortisol from your stressful day at work. Sometimes, your self-reflection and self-care can come too late, after you've already infected others with your stress.

Says one former nonprofit development director who asked us not to use her name, "When I was under extreme stress, I would come home and yell at my husband and my kids. This was really bad because my inability to do something about my stress ended my marriage."

This is not an isolated case. In a report titled "Work-Home Interference Contributes to Burnout" in the *Journal of Occupational and Environmental Medicine*, researchers suggest that, "conflicts between work and home—in both directions—are an important contributor to the risk of burnout." In addition to recommendations for employers to reduce work demands interfering with employees' private lives, the researchers also recommend that employees "develop self-regulation strategies to [counter] negative spillover of work at home, such as not working from home."[13]

For the burned-out development director, after leaving her job, her road out of burnout to revitalization included turning to her community. "I'm not a religious person," she explains. "But I am spiritual, and I found that connecting with others at my church was a big factor in helping me change my situation."

Sometimes, being with others actually relieves stress. Sandra Bass, PhD, assistant dean of students and director at the University of California Berkeley Public Service Center, says, "Often when I get stressed I want to be left alone. But sometimes the best thing you can do is be in community with other people."

The philosophy about reaching out to your community as part of self-care is embedded in her organization where students are encouraged to practice it.

"We work with over 100 student activists and leaders who, in turn, work with hundreds of other students and community organizations pursuing social justice work," says Bass. "We train and coach students that self-care is not just self-awareness but is a part of community caring. When they are stressed, they need to be in community. We create an environment for that to happen."

Turn to your friends, family, or community as sounding boards, not to hear your complaints about work but to help you assess your options for mitigating job burnout. How you relate to those closest to you can be the difference between a tense and angst-ridden transition from work to home and one of positive encouragement and nurturing support. While the Wellness Triad of sleep, nutrition, and exercise nourishes your body and brain, positive relationships with your family and friends can be nourishing to your heart and spirit.

SPHERE 3: RELATIONSHIP TO ENVIRONMENT

Many of us work more indoors than out and confine our minds, bodies, and souls to stagnant, artificial, and often toxic environments. Because we spend so much time at work, the negative elements of our work environment can erode our health and well-being. The goal of this book is to give you actionable ideas and advice along with research and data for making positive changes in the Five Spheres of Happy Healthy Living, but environment is a tough area to affect.

While there is a lot of research and reports around the ill effects of bad environments on our health, much about the environment where we live and work is difficult to change on our own. We can make some surface modifications in an office setting such as using standing desks, better lighting, or adding plants. But the office building itself and the building materials are fairly—and probably literally—set in stone. The furniture and fixtures at the office can be changed but with varying degrees of expense and usually not by one individual. When it comes to work space, the greatest burden of addressing the Sphere of Environment is on the organization, not the individual.

SPHERE 4: RELATIONSHIP TO WORK AND MONEY

Work is how you spend your time earning a living. Work can consume your life. Too often, people work just to make money to pay bills. Then if good spending and saving habits aren't in place, a vicious cycle of stress ensues. Low pay common to the nonprofit sector can exacerbate the problem.

Sphere 4 addresses *how* you work and even *why* you work. We are all working far more than we are doing almost anything else in our daily existence. "The American Time Use Survey" (2014)[14] found that during an average workday, people between 25 and 54 years of age who were employed and had kids spent an average of 8.9 hours working or in work-related activities—approximately one-third of the day. If you don't like your work or have troubles at work, that quickly spills over into other parts of your life.

When you work in a nonprofit, or anywhere for that matter, there are common stressors present that include the workload—or should we say work *overload*. As we've mentioned before, limited budgets for professional development, training, or career advancement at nonprofits create stress. Another cause of stress at work is how people treat one another, whether it is a bully on the board, extreme office politics, or an unsupportive boss.

As part of the research we did for this book, we asked many nonprofit professionals to share their daily experiences working at a nonprofit. What is life like during those eight-hour or more workdays? From their stories, we put together this composite of the work life of a nonprofit development director:

> My workday begins at 5:00 A.M. when my iPhone alarm goes off. My morning routine is about getting myself and my kids out the door. I'm often late because I check and respond to e-mails and lose track of time.
>
> I usually work late at night, so I'm tired in the morning and pick up a latte to pick me up before I go into the office. I never have any time to exercise in the morning.
>
> At the office, I make a triage plan of what I can actually get done on my massive to-do list. I go right into my e-mail and spend an hour chipping away at requests. Some can be done quickly, others have to wait until I can concentrate better, but that never seems to happen.
>
> Then it is time to prepare for an endless parade of back-to-back meetings, but phone calls and staff drop-ins interrupt me, so I often go into meetings unprepared. My work meetings are scheduled for an hour, but we can't seem to end early; I'm constantly distracted because I'm getting e-mail and text notifications.
>
> At lunch, I usually use my computer keyboard as a lunch tray, eating at my desk while chipping away at e-mail, madly following up on tasks from morning meetings, and trying to prep for the afternoon wave of meetings. Of course, in the morning meetings, I said yes to more things that get added to my to-do list. I was too tired to say no, and, honestly, my executive director has unrealistic expectations. I get so hungry or "hangry" by lunchtime that I can't resist the pizza or burger takeout even though I know I need to watch what I'm eating.
>
> One or two times a week, as a development director, I'm taking a donor or prospect out for lunch. These lunches are stressful because I have to be "on" all the time, and it is hard to really eat anything given that I'm talking for much of the time. I often have another round of back-to-back meetings in the afternoon. I find

> it draining, and I always need a second double latte in the afternoon, which I down with a chocolate bar or some potato chips.
>
> Most days, I leave the office around 6:00 P.M. to pick up the kids and have dinner as a family, help them with homework, and get them to bed. Around 9:00 P.M. or 10:00 P.M., I do the more focused office work from home—items that require quiet concentration like writing grant proposals or strategy work. I get revved up and need to watch some TV before I go to bed. I rarely go to bed before 1:00 A.M., waking up at 5:00 A.M. to repeat this pattern all week long.

Sound familiar? When we shared this composite profile with other nonprofit folks, they told us that the profile was right on, even if it was exaggerated to make a point.

Many nonprofit employees have a deep commitment to their work, and it demands that they do their best and give as much as possible to the organization and its clients. Add a workplace situation where senior management and the board have unrealistic expectations about the work and workload and throw in some dysfunctional relationships. Now you have a ticking time bomb of burnout ready to explode.

Work-Life Juggle, Not Balance

The idea of work-life balance is a bit of a misnomer. The reality is that most working professionals, especially those with families, will never find the perfect balance between work and personal time. There will always be an emergency call or a child's soccer game before the workday ends to make balance difficult; it simply is not possible to put a wall between your work and family life.

Instead of seeking balance, start honing your juggling skills to smoothly move from one aspect of your life to another. Your self-care practices will help you get better at this juggle, providing you with more energy to get things done. Add some strategy and planning to manage the multiple parts of your home life and work life and access all available support resources at your disposal. With care and attention, you can get closer to managing your Five Spheres with less stress.

"I know there will always be times when my family can't have as much of my time as they'd like to because of work and my other projects," says

Shai Coggins, a nonprofit technology consultant and blogger. "And work will not always take priority when my family needs me the most. I also give myself time for creative activities because they help me refuel."

In Chapter 5, we cover techniques to address your work-life juggle such as setting boundaries and knowing when to take a break.

SPHERE 5: RELATIONSHIP TO TECH

Technology makes it next to impossible to have a clearly defined work life versus personal life. Twenty years ago, you probably weren't having such an intimate relationship with your technology, and your tech use didn't blur the lines between work and home. While we are huge advocates for using technology, we want you to step back and take a holistic view of your relationship with your tech. Acknowledge there are some downsides to the nonstop accessibility and constant connectivity. The way you use—or abuse—tech tools can alter your overall happiness and health.

See if any of these symptoms sound familiar:

Physical: Neck, shoulder, back, arm, wrist, or hand pain, eyestrain, or illness caused by sedentary work
Mental: Distraction, inability to focus, obsessive/compulsive behavior, dependence, addiction, or boredom
Emotional: Nervousness, anxiety, frustration, depression, or interference with your relationships with others
Spiritual: Emptiness, loneliness, disconnection from others, or feeling lost

Even while you get many benefits from your ability to connect to so much information and so many people through the Internet and your tech devices, your human body and brain have limits to how much they can take before something literally, or figuratively, breaks.

Effects of Social Media and Mobile Phones

We can't talk about the effects of technology without delving more deeply into what our tech tools give us access to: social networks and other forms of social media. Social media gives us a near-real-time stream of information and disinformation at levels we've never before experienced. We are privy to more intimate details of not only the people whom we know personally, but also strangers who become increasingly familiar to us through their constant posts, tweets, and uploads.

Social Media Anxiety Syndrome (also referred to as Social Media Anxiety Disorder, or SMAD) is a term used by Neil Mehta, MD, in a 2011 article titled "How Physicians Can Overcome Social Media Anxiety on Twitter." SMAD is defined as "when the participation of social media affects the mental and physical well-being of an individual."[15] The constant barrage of data creates stress due to being overwhelmed, but it can also trigger emotional reactions in us based on what we see and read online.

"Problems have arisen for me personally around issues to do with managing bad news and bad press on social networks, in an environment where some people in the organization were slower to grasp the importance or magnitude of what was unfolding online in comparison to in the 'real world,'" says Jo Johnson, senior digital marketing manager at London Symphony Orchestra. "This left me unsupported at a time when I needed help and guidance and very nearly pushed me over the edge."

Johnson was left thinking that people working on the "front line of social media" may not be properly trained to manage crises.

Says Johnson, "Social networks can be unforgiving, and I worry that the mental health of those left dealing with the often very nasty messages could be affected. As social media can still sometimes be seen as the 'light-hearted' part of what we all do, this issue goes undetected until it's too late."

Many of us may suffer from an "iDisorder," says Dr. Larry Rosen, a professor of psychology at California State University, Dominguez Hills, in his 2012 book *iDisorder: Understanding Our Obsession with Technology and Overcoming Its Hold on Us*. Rosen defines iDisorder as "changes to your brain's ability to process information and your ability to relate to the world due to your daily use of media and technology resulting in signs and symptoms of psychological disorders—such as stress, sleeplessness, and a compulsive need to check in with all of your technology."[16]

With mobile phones becoming an inescapable part of our daily lives, whether at work or at home, another disorder—"iPhone Separation Anxiety," in which people do not like the idea of being away from their phones for any length of time—was identified in the study "The Extended iSelf: The Impact of iPhone Separation on Cognition, Emotion, and

Physiology" published in the *Journal of Computer-Mediated Communications*.[17] Does this mean that we should be completely chained to our mobile phones to avoid any anxiety that can negatively affect our work performance? Of course not!

If you are trying to improve your relationship with your smartphone to reduce stress, here are a few questions to ask yourself to see if you are using your device thoughtfully or compulsively:

- Where do you carry your phone? If it is in your hand so you don't miss an alert, then you have a problem.
- Do you sleep with your phone next to you? Many people do, including some of our colleagues. Put your phone away at least an hour before sleep to avoid disrupting your sleep. Checking your e-mail before you go to bed messes with your brain. Leave your phone out of the bedroom!
- Do you feel uncomfortable or anxious when your phone is not close at hand? Not being comfortable when you're away from your phone is a problem even if you try to laugh it off.
- When you eat dinner or other meals with family, friends, or colleagues, is your phone on the table, within inches of your fork? Putting your phone within view or easy reach is temptation to be distracted from the people around you. Just don't do it!

We can blame technology all we want; however, the problem is not that these devices and platforms exist or that they give us unprecedented access to information and connections. The problem is how we are using them without paying attention or noticing that our tech habits have shifted from occasional use to mindless use. In Chapter 4, we offer techniques to temper your addictive or compulsive tech habits and to help you to stop sleeping with your smartphone!

IT'S TIME TO MAKE A CHANGE

You may feel overwhelmed by all the areas in your life where you should practice self-care and change your habits to improve your well-being. Even though there are only five Spheres of Happy Healthy Living, they are big spheres. Where and how do you start? What habits do you need to change? How do you create a plan to change them? We'll address all of this and more next.

CHAPTER 3

The Assessments

Change Your Habits, Make a Self-Care Plan

I believe "snapped self-assessment quiz clipboard in half with bare hands" is a 3.8 on the Scacella-Turgemeyer Stress Scale.

SELF-ASSESSMENT IS THE FIRST STEP

Honest and thoughtful self-assessment can help you identify bad habits you need to change and good habits you should adopt to bring you to a happier, healthier way of living and working. By doing so, you will learn what you need to do to have more energy and focus, and you will develop stress-coping mechanisms to work better, not harder, on your organization's mission.

The assessments and checklists in this chapter can help you examine your stress symptoms and triggers, understand your current self-care practices (or lack thereof), and get a better picture of your overall well-being. Carve out some quiet time to go through these assessments. Think of this time as a gift of self-care you give yourself that will keep on giving for years to come!

After reviewing numerous nonprofit assessment instruments, we developed a new set based on the ideas and frameworks in this book. In some cases, we point you to existing references online. You can download printable PDF versions of each of our assessments at www.happyhealthynonprofit.org.

1. *The Nonprofit Burnout Assessment:* A rating system to help you recognize whether you are on the path to burnout or not. Note: This is not a medical or mental health diagnostic tool.
2. *Your Current Reactions to Stress:* An often-used assessment to examine your negative and positive behaviors in response to stress.
3. *Current Self-Care Behaviors and Stress Triggers Reflection Worksheet:* An addendum to the previous assessment to help you reflect on your reactions to stress.
4. *Individual Self-Care Assessment and Checklists:* Checklists with a rating system to assess your self-care habits and practices organized by the Five Spheres of Happy Healthy Living.

Look for patterns in your responses about how you address self-care. Do you completely ignore it? Are you better with attending to some spheres but not great with others? Our hope is that through greater awareness of any problem areas, you can make deliberate choices to better attend to your self-care. Attending to your self-care will send positive ripple effects throughout all of your spheres and inoculate you against many of the stressors we've outlined in this book.

The Nonprofit Burnout Assessment

In Chapter 1, we introduced you to the four steps to nonprofit burnout that identify different phases of burnout in terms of loss of passion for your mission. The following assessment can help you become more aware of your stress symptoms and identify where you fall on the Nonprofit Passion Continuum before burnout takes its toll.

Note: This assessment is not a clinical diagnostic instrument and is provided for informational purposes only. If you have any concerns about your state of physical or mental health, consult with a medical professional.

How to Use This Tool

Review each statement and place an X in the column that best scores the frequency with which you identify with each feeling described.

Use this scale:

0 = Not at all

1 = Rarely

2 = Sometimes

3 = Often

4 = Very Often

Statements	0	1	2	3	4
Physical and Emotional					
I feel run down and drained of physical or emotional energy.					
I have trouble sleeping at night.					
I get aches and pains and other physical symptoms.					
I have a loss of appetite or overeat/drink unhealthy foods.					
I have trouble paying attention and concentrating on important tasks.					
I am forgetful.					
I feel anxiety, depression, or anger toward work.					
Signs of Cynicism and Detachment					
I have negative thoughts about my work.					
I have less empathy with coworkers or clients than they deserve.					
I am easily annoyed and irritated by problems or by my coworkers or clients.					
I feel that I am not fulfilled doing my job.					
I feel less curiosity, excitement, joy, passion, or hope about my work.					
I feel misunderstood or unappreciated at work.					
I feel I have no one I can talk to.					

(*continued*)

Statements	0	1	2	3	4
Signs of Ineffectiveness and Lack of Accomplishment					
I feel I am not learning anything new at work or gaining new skills.					
I feel I am achieving less than I should.					
I feel tremendous unpleasant pressure to succeed.					
I feel I am in the wrong profession or organization.					
I am frustrated or bored with my job.					
I feel overwhelmed at work with all I have to get done.					
I feel I do not have enough time to do many of the tasks that are important to doing a high-quality job.					
I feel I do not have enough planning time.					
TOTAL					

Now tally up the number of 1s, 2s, 3s, and 4s you've marked. Add all numbers together until you have a single score. Once you have your total, find where you fall in the Nonprofit Passion Continuum below.

Step 1: Passion Driven
Score: 0–22

You still have a passionate belief in the cause and your organization's mission. If you are working harder because of limited resources, your idealism, energy, and positive attitude will only carry you so far. You may get away with not having a solid self-care plan for a while, but having one in place will help you sustain your passion.

Step 2: Passion Waning
Score: 23–44

You're not yet in a state of emergency, but this stage can be deceiving. If you dismiss any stress you might be experiencing as insignificant, you begin to tip the scales toward burning out. Examine your behaviors. If you respond to stress with negative behaviors, start making better choices to enhance your well-being. Do not self-sacrifice and neglect setting up a self-care plan. Get started with changing habits now.

Step 3: Passion Challenged
Score: 45–66

At this stage, a self-care plan is mission-critical to improving your well-being and reigniting your passion. You may not be able to control the stress that is affecting you, but you can start controlling how you react. Consult a medical or mental health professional about any physical symptoms or signs of stress or depression you are experiencing.

Step 4: Passion Depleted
Score: 67–88

Get help now! You are one step away from self-destruction. See a medical or mental health professional immediately about your physical symptoms or signs of stress or depression. Once you get professional health care guidance, return to this book and assemble your self-care plan to support your return to well-being.

We're sure we don't have to tell you that mostly 0s and 1s are good but mostly 3s and 4s are bad or that being at Step 1 is admirable but Step 4 should be setting off emergency alarms, and you better be dialing your health care professional right now. The next assessments and checklists can help you better pinpoint why you're at a particular stage and shine some light on areas that need your care and attention.

Your Current Reactions to Stress

Self-care can minimize your stress and act as an antidote to many of the stressors that you may face each day working at a nonprofit. The next assessment comes from the University of Buffalo School of Social Work Self-Care Kit.[1] The source is unknown, but it is used by many nonprofits, including Crisis Text Line.[2]

How to Use

Put an X to signify "Yes" you engage in the behavior or "No" you don't. Pay attention to any tendency you might have toward self-deception. The truth might be ugly or embarrassing, but use it as your catalyst for change.

When you are under stress, do you:	**Yes**	**No**	**When you are under stress, do you:**	**Yes**	**No**
Smoke/use tobacco			Engage in physical activity at least three times a week for 30 minutes		
Consume more than two to three cups of caffeinated drinks per day			Get seven to nine hours of sleep per night		

(continued)

When you are under stress, do you:	Yes	No	When you are under stress, do you:	Yes	No
Drink more than one to two alcoholic beverages per day			Maintain healthy alcoholic drinking habits—if any		
Misuse over the counter medications			Find time to relax throughout your day/ week as needed		
Misuse prescription medications			Meditate		
Participate in illegal drug use			Find different ways to manage stress		
Overeat or undereat			Maintain healthy eating habits		
Spend too much money			Maintain healthy rituals and routines		
Engage in risky sexual behavior			Maintain relationships with family or friends		
Sleep too much			Walk in the woods		
Have angry outbursts			Find ways to manage your anger		
Blame yourself for anything that goes wrong			Practice positive self-talk		
Overwork or underwork			Play		
Stay silent about problems			Verbalize what you're struggling with in a professional manner		
Other			Other		
NEGATIVE SELF-CARE BEHAVIORS TALLY			**POSITIVE SELF-CARE BEHAVIORS TALLY**		

The purpose of this exercise is help you assess any negative self-care behaviors that might be increasing your stress levels, leading to burnout. If you answer more "Yeses" in the left column than the right column, then you are choosing to react to your stress in negative ways. Think about ways you can replace your negative stress reactions and behaviors with more positive ones Hint: Self-care activities are a good start. The checklists later in this chapter can help you identify a whole range of self-care practices available to you as alternative ways of dealing with your stress.

Stress Triggers and Self-Care Behaviors Worksheet

Doing a candid assessment of whether you handle your stress in a productive or destructive way can help you identify habits to change for your self-care plan. In the previous assessment, you identified whether you engage in positive or negative self-care behaviors in response to stress. Your next step is to keep a diary of your stress triggers and make a note about how you tend to respond to them. This exercise can help you gain more self-awareness about how to manage your stress, anticipate stressful situations, and identify bad habits you need to change.

Stress Trigger	**Self-Care Behavior**	**Negative or Positive?**	**If negative, what positive behavior can you replace it with?**

Download this worksheet from www.happyhealthynonprofit.org for an easy-to-fill-out version.

Happy, Healthy Nonprofit: Individual Self-Care Assessment and Checklists

Mark the following checklists to assess your self-care practices based on the Five Spheres of Happy Healthy Living. The self-care plan that you create for yourself should be customized to fit your own needs and personality. Use the time you spend going through the lists below to highlight actions that resonate with you to include in your self-care plan. Assemble a mix of things you can do in the morning, throughout the day, and at night. In Chapters 4 and 5, we share stories from nonprofit professionals who provide specific self-care practices you can adopt at work and home. This assessment and accompanying checklists were inspired by the Self-Care Starter Kit from the University of Buffalo.

How to Use

Think about each positive behavior. Rate for frequency—how often you practice each self-care habit—and for your motivation—how interested you are in doing them? We recommend going through the lists first rating for frequency then take another pass rating for motivation. Fill in "other" if you think of related activities you already do or can do.

As you go through the lists, use a highlighting pen to mark the practices that you've rated with a + (really want to do this). Sometimes, it can be easier to start with things you are motivated to do rather than the must do's. You've got to start somewhere!

Rating for Frequency

3 = I practice this self-care habit daily or almost daily.
2 = I practice this self-care habit occasionally.
1 = I practice this self-care habit once in a blue moon.
0 = I never do this.

Rating for Motivation

? = Never thought about doing this.
! = I really need to do this.
+ = I really want to do this.
* = I would never do this or it would be very difficult for me to make it a habit.

Sphere 1: Relationship to Self Checklist

How you relate to and take care of yourself makes up your first sphere. Without prioritizing self-care, all other spheres suffer or fall apart. Here are ways you can attend to your personal well-being across different areas of your whole self.

Physical Health

_Get regular medical care for prevention
_Seek medical or dental care when needed
_Don't go into work when sick
_Get enough sleep
_Be sexual
_Eat healthily
_Attend to personal hygiene
_Wear clothing I like
_Get massages
_Exercise
_Stretch
_Dance
_Take a hike or walk in nature
_Go swimming or soak in a hot tub
_Play a sport
_Engage in a fun physical activity
_Take three deep breaths anytime during the day
_Get 15 minutes of sunshine
Other:

Downtime

_Don't work on weekends
_Schedule regular downtime
_Take a nap
_Take real vacations
_Take day trips or mini-vacations
_Go for a drive without a destination in mind
_Make time for self-reflection
_Enjoy escape entertainment—movie, sports event, crafts fair
_Make time to keep up with home chores: laundry, dusting, vacuuming, or lawn work

Mind

_Set personal improvement goals for myself
_Read books or articles not related to work
_Do something new or that I'm not an expert in
_Take a class that engages my mind and is not work-related such as a cooking or art class, etc.
_Engage my mind in a new area such as going to a concert, museum, theater
_Listen to music
_Sing out loud
_Do crossword puzzles or play word games
_Use a brain training or memory app
_Be curious
Other:

Emotions

_Set boundaries with toxic or negative people
_Understand who and what pushes my buttons
_Manage situations when people do push my buttons
_Give myself affirmations
_Love myself
_Allow myself to cry
_Laugh out loud
_Channel my outrage through social action, letters, donations, etc.
_Pay attention to my inner dialogue, self-talk, feelings, etc.
_Keep a gratitude journal
Other:

(*continued*)

_Engage in a regular hobby I enjoy like gardening, cooking, baking, crafting _Play a game like a card game or board game _Play with a child or a baby Other: **Mindfulness** _Eat slowly _Meditate _Try a meditation app _Yoga _Try a yoga app _Pay attention to my breathing _Spend time watching the clouds _Quietly and closely examine a flower Other: **Creativity** _Color with adult coloring books _Color with a child _Try meditative art like Zentangle _Doodle _Sketch or follow a YouTube video on sketching _Make music _Play with air dry clay or Play-Doh _Weave a friendship bracelet _String beads Other:	**Spiritual Self-Care** _Make time for quiet reflection _Spend time in nature _Find a spiritual connection or community _Be open to inspiration _Be optimistic and hopeful _Be aware of nonmaterial aspects of my life _Be open to not knowing _Identify what is meaningful to me and notice its place in my life _Learn more about my religion _Learn more about another religion _Pray _Read or listen to inspirational talks, music Other:

Sphere 2: Relationship to Others Checklist

Your relationships with family, friends, and acquaintances off-line and online make up your second sphere. In life and at work, you cannot avoid interacting with others. Your behaviors, habits, and well-being affect and influence others, and the reverse is true as well. Here are ways you can attend to your relationships.

Relationship with Family	Relationship with Friends
_Schedule regular dates with my partner or spouse _Schedule regular activities with my children	_Stay in contact with friends near and far _Stay in contact with important people in my life _Write a letter, put it in an envelope, and mail it _Schedule time to reply thoughtfully to personal e-mails

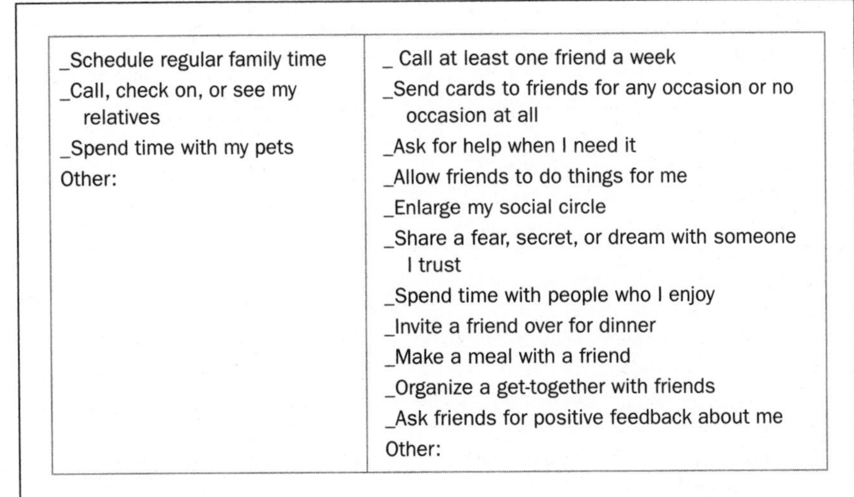

_Schedule regular family time _Call, check on, or see my relatives _Spend time with my pets Other:	_ Call at least one friend a week _Send cards to friends for any occasion or no occasion at all _Ask for help when I need it _Allow friends to do things for me _Enlarge my social circle _Share a fear, secret, or dream with someone I trust _Spend time with people who I enjoy _Invite a friend over for dinner _Make a meal with a friend _Organize a get-together with friends _Ask friends for positive feedback about me Other:

Sphere 3: Relationship to Environment Checklist

The environment around you makes up your third sphere. Environment is a major force in your life, but you may not be aware of its tremendous affect on you every day. While you may not be able to significantly change your environment, you can make small changes, like those listed below, to create a cleaner, safer space for yourself to improve your health and well-being.

Your Home and Office	**Outdoors**
_Declutter your home _Declutter your desk _Clean something in your house you've avoided cleaning _Change your lightbulbs to softer, energy efficient ones _Add plants to your home or office _Plant an indoor or outdoor garden _Use an ionic air cleaner _Use an aromatherapy diffuser (note coworker allergies) Other:	_Walk outside at least once a day _Spend time at a lake, river, pool, or other body of water _Find a hiking trail near you and explore _Take a different route to work _Ride a bike _Go to a park or a zoo Other:

Sphere 4: Relationship to Work and Money Checklist

Your fourth sphere takes up a lot of your time and attention and can cause stress when you don't have good boundaries and emotions around work and money. Caring for your work relationships and caring for yourself while at work can vastly enhance your well-being. Here are some ways to do just that.

(continued)

Workplace Self-Care	Life/Work Juggling
_Take a lunch break away from desk during the workday _Take time to chat with coworkers _Make quiet time to complete tasks _Understand my energy levels and plan work day accordingly _Understand my concentration levels and plan workday accordingly _Get help from coworkers or boss when needed _Don't answer e-mail all day _Identify projects and tasks that are exciting and rewarding _Have a system for effectively managing time and workload _Set limits with clients, colleagues, and coworkers _Balance my workload so I'm not overloaded every day _Arrange my workspace so it is comforting _Negotiate for my needs (benefits, pay raise, workload, comp time) _Take comp time when earned _Don't do work when I am on vacation _Take weekends off _Have a professional peer group from which to get support or inspiration _Invest in professional development to learn new work skills on a regular basis Other:	_Strive to juggle work, family, and personal activities _Strive to juggle work and family time _Strive to juggle work and work life Other: **Relationship with Money** _See a financial adviser to map out a financial plan _Open up and use a savings account _ Use software like Mint to get a dashboard view of my finances _Cut back on frivolous spending _Bring lunch to work Other:

Sphere 5: Relationship to Tech Checklist

Navigating the new sphere of your relationship with your technology can be challenging because you may already have developed bad habits around your tech. Here are some ways to implement tech wellness.

Getting Away from Tech	Technology Self-Care
_Take technology mini-detoxes or breaks when needed _Unplug from work e-mail and social media on vacations _Unplug from work e-mail and social media on weekends	_Use a standing desk _Regularly stop, stand, and stretch away from the computer _Get a glare shield for my computer screen _Get an ergonomic keyboard

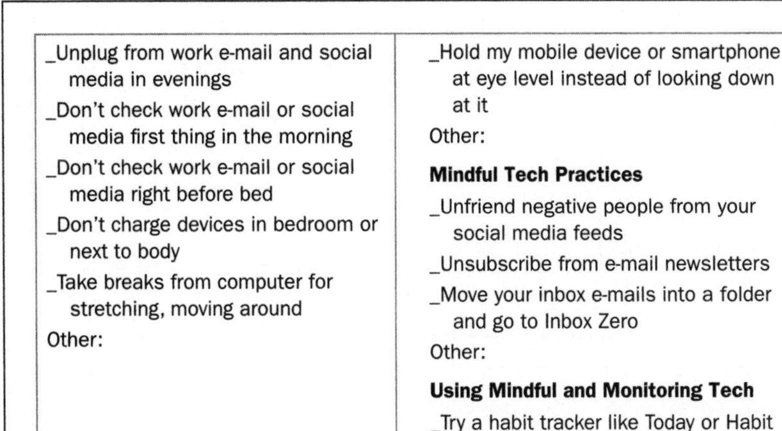

_Unplug from work e-mail and social media in evenings

_Don't check work e-mail or social media first thing in the morning

_Don't check work e-mail or social media right before bed

_Don't charge devices in bedroom or next to body

_Take breaks from computer for stretching, moving around

Other:

_Hold my mobile device or smartphone at eye level instead of looking down at it

Other:

Mindful Tech Practices

_Unfriend negative people from your social media feeds

_Unsubscribe from e-mail newsletters

_Move your inbox e-mails into a folder and go to Inbox Zero

Other:

Using Mindful and Monitoring Tech

_Try a habit tracker like Today or Habit List

_Install RescueTime on my computer to track my productivity

_Use the Moment app to monitor how often I check my phone

_Use the Human app or FitBolt web browser plugin to remind me to get up and move around

Other:

Congratulations! You made it through the assessments, worksheets, and checklists. Self-assessment is like holding a mirror to your life. While sometimes you might not like what you see, it gives you the opportunity to change your habits and improve your attitude and behaviors.

CREATING CHANGE

Self-assessment is just the beginning of the process for initiating change. Now that you've spent some time with the tools in this chapter, you should have identified the following:

1. Your stress triggers
2. Bad response habits that you should address
3. Good response habits that you should continue to do
4. Where you may need to set boundaries at work
5. New self-care practices that you can adopt to build routines or habits

To put the results of these exercises into action, you may need to change some habits. We know that's not easy to do. In the next section of this chapter, we'll explain why habit change is difficult and how to get around it.

Attitude Changes (Mind-Set)

Take a hard look at the bad habits you need to change, and examine your lack of established good habits. Both are depleting your crucial energy to do your work well. Later in this book, we explore how organizations can support you and others at your nonprofit in making positive changes for more sustainable focus, motivation, and productivity. But let's start with you.

All the habit-change experts will tell you, changing habits is challenging but possible. First, you need to understand how habit formation works to develop an effective habit-changing process for yourself. In his book, *The Power of Habit: Why We Do What We Do in Life and Business*, Pulitzer Prize–winning *New York Times* reporter Charles Duhigg talks about the three steps of habit formation—also called the "Habit Loop:"[3]

1. Cue: the trigger of a particular behavior. This could be an alarm clock that initiates your wake-up routine or seeing something like a sign or Post-it note or any other catalyst for action.
2. Routine: the process of acting on the cue—physically, mentally, even emotionally. When the routine becomes automatic, it is a habit.
3. Reward: something that signals to your brain, "Yes, remember this routine," reinforcing it as a habit.

Duhigg also refers to "chunking," the process when your brain converts a sequence of actions into an automatic routine—a routine you don't have to think about because it is now a "behavioral chunk" or habit. Forming a new habit, or getting rid of an old one, requires reminders and repetition and takes time.

Behavior Changes (Actions)

You can't separate your attitudes toward habits and habit change from your actual habits or behaviors. Understanding your attitude, or even your personality type, can be helpful as you work toward changing your behaviors. We love author Gretchen Rubin's take on habit change. Rubin examines what she calls "Four Tendencies" in her book *Better Than Before* and lays out scenarios to help you determine which one of the Four Tendencies or attitudes you have toward outer and inner expectations. Then she lays out ways to change your own habits once you know your Tendency.

The Four Tendencies

1. Upholder. Meets outer (from other people) and inner (from self) expectations.
2. Questioner. Resists outer expectations (often by questioning everything) but meets inner ones. If an expectation makes sense to them, they treat it more like an inner one.
3. Obliger. Meets outer expectations (think: people pleaser) but resists inner ones (doing for others before doing for themselves).
4. Rebel. Resists outer and inner expectations. Bucks the system.[4]

Your Tendency influences the approach you need to take if you want to change a habit. For example, if you are an Upholder, chances are changing or adopting a habit is much easier than if you are a Questioner questioning the reasons for changing or a Rebel not doing what is expected. Knowing your Tendency—the internal aspect of yourself that influences your behavior—is a critical element of habit change. We highly recommend Rubin's book to get to the bottom of your nature to better handle habit change.

What causes behavioral change? Scientist B.J. Fogg came up with The Fogg Behavior Model[5] that breaks down how behavior happens: first there is *motivation* or the desire to act, followed by the *ability* to carry out the particular behavior, and then some kind of *trigger* or cue so the behavior takes place, like a call to action or a reminder.

When setting a habit, you may not be successful because the habit is too big or you didn't identify the right trigger. The key to changing habits, according to Fogg, is to iterate on the habit or trigger until you find the right mix that helps you make a smaller change.

Fogg also talks about "Six Elements of Simplicity" or six things that might block your ability to create a new habit:

1. Time
2. Money

3. Physical effort
4. Brain cycles (mental effort)
5. Social deviance
6. Nonroutine

Without simplicity, habits are hard to adopt. We've talked a lot already about the essential nature of self-care for your holistic well-being—for your mind, body, spirit, and emotions. Let's take a look at acts of self-care through the lens of Fogg's Six Elements of Simplicity:

1. Time. Self-care takes time, but even small amounts of time devoted to self-care can bring great benefits, such as five minutes of meditation a day instead of one hour.
2. Money. Self-care doesn't have to cost anything. You can move into a yoga pose several times a day and get benefits without having to pay for an ongoing class. Or you can encourage your organization to incorporate a yoga class into the workweek that is free of charge.
3. Physical effort. You don't have to push yourself to do strenuous exercise but instead incorporate simple stretches into short breaks throughout your workday.
4. Brain cycles (mental effort). The beauty of self-care is that it doesn't take a lot of mental effort and, when practiced regularly, actually revitalizes your brain and refreshes your mind.
5. Social deviance. Self-care is not socially deviant—but it isn't taken as seriously as it should be. Self-care produces scientifically proven benefits and combats a whole host of work-related and technology-related ailments so should qualify as socially acceptable and socially essential.
6. Nonroutine.Things that are not a routine are hard to adopt. Self-care activities must become routine as a practice or a series of repeated rituals to sustain over the long term and for you to experience large and lasting benefits.

Let's face it: knowing about self-care doesn't translate into doing self-care. Doing self-care requires habit change. Likewise, having self-care resources available to you in your home and at your workplace isn't enough to ensure you actually use them. Using them requires habit change, and habit change requires simplicity for it to really take hold.

Habit Changes (Sustaining)

Even if you understand the habits you need to adopt or change, even if you have the right attitude, and even if you know the right steps to take to make a change in your behavior, that change might not last. To have sustained habit change, you need motivation. According to Daniel Pink,[6] the carrot/stick model of reward and punishment just doesn't work when it comes to motivation. He says there are three main factors that motivate us to do anything:

1. Autonomy. This is the desire to be self-directed, to have some independence and ownership.
2. Mastery. This is the urge to keep improving at something that is important to us.
3. Purpose. This is the sense that what we do serves a purpose beyond ourselves.

B.J. Fogg identified three things that change behavior long term:[7]

1. Option A. Have an epiphany.
2. Option B. Change your environment (what surrounds you).
3. Option C. Take baby steps.

Fogg jokes that having an epiphany—some kind of mystical experience—is rare, so your real options for long-term behavioral change are to change your environment or to take baby steps or both. For sustainable behavior change, you need the right conditions so the behavior becomes more automatic and less of a chore. To keep it going, you need fundamental environment change and an easy process—the baby steps.

Beth participated in a five-day process that Fogg offers online for free that has helped thousands of people change habits using his Tiny Habits method.[8] What she learned from Fogg's method is the habit anyone wants to establish has to be really small and specific. If you find yourself not taking that first step toward changing a habit, you should evaluate the size of your habit and revise it, making it smaller.

Beth wanted to start a new habit of meditation:

When I get up in the morning, I will meditate.

The first day, she didn't do it.

After reflecting on both the trigger and the goal, she came up with something smaller and more specific:

> When I sit down at my computer for work, I will close my eyes for three minutes and breathe deeply while the computer is booting up.

This shift got her started, and now she does a quiet meditation for 10 minutes each day before she starts working.

Gretchen Rubin identifies these three pillars for sustainable positive change:

1. Monitoring: Measure, track, and reflect on your behavior.
2. Scheduling: Put the first step of your new habit or behavior change into your calendar so you actually take that first step.
3. Accountability: Bring someone else into the process with you or build in more public check-ins so others can help keep you on track.[9]

Rubin also identifies the four foundation habits that can help with any attempts at habit change:

1. Getting enough sleep
2. Getting some exercise
3. Creating external order
4. Managing eating and drinking

Do you recognize the Wellness Triad in there? Without fortifying your foundation for habit change, your changes won't be as sustainable as you'd like. Be constantly vigilant for any internal or external forces that get in the way of keeping up with a good habit that you're trying to form or sustain.

MAKING IT HAPPEN: YOUR SELF-CARE ACTION PLAN

We hold on to many of our bad habits and bad behaviors because we are completely unaware that we are doing them. Or we know we are doing them but are unaware of the damage they are causing. Or we know the damage they are causing, but it is the way we've always done things or the effort to stop doing them or doing something differently seems overwhelming. Or maybe we don't know where to begin. Or we know where to begin, but we just can't get around to taking the first step.

The reasons for not changing our work and lives for the better are endless, but the excuses must stop here. Luckily, there are small and simple changes you can make that will make a major difference in your work and life over both the short and long term. Many of these actions you can take are part of the big bucket of goodness of self-care. Let's talk about how to organize these actions into a plan.

Creating Your Self-Care Plan

A self-care plan identifies self-care goals or behaviors that you want to sustain and is your strategy for making positive behaviors routine with some form of accountability. Self-care is something that you need to live and practice daily. Schedule your self-care activities. Put them on your calendar. Make a commitment to yourself, and prioritize self-care as mission-critical.

A written self-care plan spells out daily activities that will reduce your stress and revitalize you. Writing down your plan helps you articulate and define your routines and rituals for self-care. The goal is to help prevent and potentially eliminate the destructive impact of chronic stress. Self-care is meant to help you cope better in the face of workplace stress and life challenges. A self-care plan is your road map to happy and healthy.

Your self-care practices are personal and particular to your needs, preferences, personality, and motivation. Some of the basics of self-care are essential, and you should not shirk them, like getting enough rest, eating healthy foods, exercising, and making space for downtime. But the specific practices you integrate into your life around your relationships, spirituality, and any of the other areas is entirely up to you. If you feel that you don't have a creative bone in your body, then meditative art as a mindfulness activity might not be your cup of tea. Maybe taking a dance or stretching class is a better fit or simply starting a regular walking routine. Don't judge yourself or let others judge you for the self-care choices you make—as long as they are grounded in happy and healthy principals.

Self-Care Plan Templates

A written self-care plan does not have to be a long document. In fact, the shorter the better to start. You can always add to it as you progress through your self-care practices. Make a list of your practice goals or the specific actions you plan on taking to attend to your self-care. Tie your actions to the Five Spheres of Happy Healthy Living, and identify only a few practices related to each category.

Here is an example of a basic self-care plan:

Self-Care Category	Practice Goals
Sphere 1: Self	-Get seven to nine hours of sleep per night. -Eat more fruits and vegetables every day. -Get to 10,000 steps per day walking.
Sphere 2: Others	-Make a regular date with my partner and/or children—one-on-one—to give my relationships attention. -Divest myself of negative influences, moving consciously away from people who bring me down.
Sphere 3: Environment	-Stop what I'm doing at least once a day to go outside. -Check my home and office for toxic materials and chemicals that can be eliminated and bring in healthier alternatives.
Sphere 4: Work and Money	-Take comp time when I'm attending work-related evening events. -Stand up from my desk every 15 minutes to stretch and walk around.
Sphere 5: Tech	-Set up a charging station at the front door for all of my/my family's digital devices. -Keep all my digital devices out of my bedroom and off my dinner table.

You might be all fired up and ready to get started, but if this plan feels overwhelming, pare it down to one practice per area or several practices in just one area and stick to them for a month. The following month, add a little more and so on. You might even consider identifying a monthly theme and commit to a year of establishing self-care habits as a framework for your plan.

Your plan could look like this:

Month	Self-Care Category	Practice Goals
January	Sphere 1: Self	Get seven to nine hours of sleep per night.
February	Sphere 2: Others	Make a regular date with my partner and/or children—one-on-one—to give my relationships attention.
March	Sphere 3: Environment	Stop what I'm doing at least once a day to go outside.
April	Sphere 4: Work and Money	Stand up from my desk every 15 minutes to stretch and walk around.
May	Sphere 5: Tech	Set up a charging station at the front door for all of my/my family's digital devices.

Or it could look like this:

Month	Practice Goals
January	Get seven to nine hours of sleep per night.
February	Eat more fruits and vegetables every day.
March	Get to 10,000 steps a day walking.
April	Make a regular date with my partner and/or children —one-on-one—to give my relationships attention.
May	Divest myself of negative influences, moving consciously away from people who bring me down.
June	Stop what I'm doing at least once a day to go outside.

Roll your self-care plan out slowly and deliberately.

Another format for a self-care plan is based around your Self-Care Bill of Rights. List your "rights" to self-care, and then add some concrete action steps to implement them. For example, taking a cue from Aisha Moore's Self-Care Bill of Rights, here is what your plan might look like:

I have the right to:	I will do this:	Target Date:
Put my mental, physical, emotional, and spiritual health above everything and everyone else	Say "no" more often when asked to do things beyond my capacity and set better boundaries at work	As often as possible
Give to others and this world in a way that energizes me	Identify a local charity to donate to or volunteer some of my time	This quarter
Adequate sleep	Go to bed 30 minutes earlier	Now
Focus on my physical body and outward appearance	Make an appointment with an image consultant	This month
Pamper myself	Take an aromatherapy class	This quarter

Get even more compact using B.J. Fogg's Tiny Habits method and do only this one thing starting today:

Get seven to nine hours of sleep every night.

Once you have established a better sleep routine and are feeling the benefits from it, then do this:

Eat more fruits and vegetables every day.

You get the picture. Put your one tiny habit into your daily calendar and create reminders—triggers or cues such as an alarm on your iPhone, a Post-it note on your bathroom mirror or refrigerator door. or a friend checking in with you.

Even when you write down and schedule your self-care goals and practices, they may need to be tweaked as you learn more about yourself. Changing habits and incorporating self-care into your work and life are iterative processes. Identify what isn't working and get rid of it. Find what works for you and stick with it.

Tips for Self-Care

Doing what is good for you doesn't have to be hard. If you use the approach of starting with small steps and adding on incrementally, you can build a solid, steady practice. To better adopt your self-care practices, don't just write out your plan but also track your progress and revisit your plan and outcomes on a regular basis.

Additional tips for carrying out your self-care plan include:

- Keep your written self-care plan in a place where you can see it every day. Keeping it visible will help you to think about and commit to the strategies in your plan.
- Make a laminated abbreviated version of your Self-Care Bill of Rights and carry it with you in your wallet, purse, or bag.
- Share your self-care plan with a trusted colleague, friend, or family member so he or she can support you in your actions—your accountability buddy.
- Stick to your plan and practice the activities regularly. Just like an athlete doesn't become fit by merely thinking about fitness, you can't expect to perform effectively without putting into practice a holistic plan for your well-being.
- Reassess how you are doing at the end of one month and then three months. Behaviors can take over a month to become habits, so check in and be realistic. After a while, come back and complete the self-care assessments in this chapter again to see how well you are doing with your new, improved habits.
- Be gentle with yourself. If you fail to carry out a new self-care routine, try to assess why. You may need to make the thing you're trying to change smaller and more manageable. Don't beat yourself up about not meeting your goals. But don't stop trying to meet at least one goal at a time.

The next two chapters are filled with self-care tips and techniques you can apply directly to your Five Spheres of Happy Healthy Living.

CHAPTER 4

The Practices

Happy, Healthy Things You Can Do for Yourself

I'm doing the picture of the nonprofit staffer now. Do you have a color that says "totally stressed and burned out"?

INDIVIDUAL SELF-CARE

You don't live in a vacuum. Everyone you encounter benefits from your self-care. Imagine how much more effective you and your nonprofit could be if you took care of yourself as you take care of those your organization serves. Imagine what it would be like if you were able to access energy or calm as needed when you did your work or lived your life. Pay attention to your Five Spheres of Happy Healthy Living (self, others, environment, work and money, and tech). We can't talk about self-care for you as an individual without acknowledging how you fit into the world and how you interact with everything and everyone around you.

Incorporating self-care into your day and your work reinforces the good habits that help fortify you against stress. A whole, well person is better able to tackle the day's challenges with more focus, vibrancy, and perseverance. Let's hear from other nonprofit professionals to see why, when, and how they fit self-care into their days—and nights.

SUPPORTING HEALTH AND WELLNESS

We've shared the studies, reports, and statistics that support the importance of attending to your sleep, nutrition, and fitness. Now let's look at the practical applications and practices that address the Wellness Triad from other nonprofit professionals as well as other ways to bring self-care into your everyday life outside of work.

Wellness Triad: Sleeping

Cheating yourself out of a good night's sleep can harm your well-being. The good news is you can make small and incremental changes that can have a big impact on the quality and quantity of your sleep. Nonprofit consultant Joyce Lee-Ibarra monitored her own sleep habits and made some concrete changes to improve her sleep quality. One simple change she made was leaving her iPhone outside her bedroom at night to get better rest with less temptation for distraction. Lee-Ibarra says that better sleep has helped her reduce the cluttered brain feeling she gets when trying to fall asleep at night.

Without electronic distractions, Lee-Ibarra falls asleep with less stress. She is also reducing the disruptions to her circadian rhythm that can be caused by the light from digital screens. Circadian rhythms are 24-hour cycles that all living beings go through, usually based on daylight in daytime and dark at nighttime. Staying awake until sunrise can disrupt your circadian rhythm and confuse your brain. Using your electronic devices before bedtime can trick your brain into waking just as you're trying to fall asleep, leading to less rest and more stress.

Lee-Ibarra recommends two specific tips for getting better sleep:

1. Unplug an hour before bedtime.
2. Find a relaxing routine to establish before you go to bed. For her, reading is relaxing, but she says for others, it might be meditating, taking a bath, drinking a cup of tea, and the like.

We both have modified our own nighttime habits to create better conditions for restful sleep. Beth replaced her iPhone with a Moonbeam alarm clock, eliminating temptation to check her phone in bed at night. Aliza established a "no electronics in the bedroom" policy for her entire family. Both of us also use meditative art as a relaxation technique before bedtime with good results. We'll talk more about that later in this chapter.

Leadership coach Lolly Daskal, of the company Lead from Within, recommends waking earlier to set the tone for a more successful and less stressful day. In her blog post, "Success Is a Sunrise Away,"[1] Daskal explains that early risers have more time in the morning to exercise if they want, or read, meditate, or pray. Researchers at the University of Barcelona in Spain[2] found that early risers could better resist fatigue and frustration, experience less anxiety, and lower rates of depression. Their research was based on circadian rhythms.

Gina C. Lynn, executive director of the Greater Rostraver Chamber of Commerce in Pennsylvania, goes to bed early and wakes up early as part of her healthy sleep practice. "I'm not ashamed to call it an early night to catch up on my zzzs or to nap on a weekend. I feel my best with eight hours per night," Lynn explains.

Even if you get a restful sleep, what you do first thing in the morning can set the tone for your day. Although Beth moved her iPhone out of her room at night, she found herself going into the kitchen first thing in the morning and looking at her work e-mail, raising her stress level before she even started work. She switched her morning routine to doing light housework like emptying the dishwasher before checking her messages and put her iPhone into a drawer, out of sight. By giving herself time to settle into her morning, she started her day with more calm.

Establishing a good night's sleep with a relaxing bedtime routine and reinforcing it with a less stressful morning ritual can be the perfect initial self-care practice. On to nutrition!

Wellness Triad: Nutrition

There are many traditional and alternative approaches to good nutrition and healthy eating. So many, in fact, it is difficult to sort through what is scientifically valid and what is bogus without a PhD, MD in nutritional medicine. If you are ready to make a change to a healthy eating lifestyle—in other words, french fries and bacon cheeseburgers for more fruits, vegetables, and whole foods—we recommend first discussing good nutrition with your doctor.

Take advantage of any resources offered by your nonprofit's health care insurance plan or HMO like nutritional coaching or classes. When Beth wanted to get on the road to a healthy diet, her doctor referred her to a local American Heart Association for its Heart Healthy Eating Nutrition Class. While it wasn't free, the class was low cost and provided Beth with coaching and guidance by experts.

Gina C. Lynn tries to eat healthy foods as part of her self-care practice:

> I feel my best when I stay away from carbs and processed food. I try to eat whole foods. I cook at home on most occasions and prepare from scratch. With my job, I often eat lunch or dinner out. I'm selective with my ordering choices.

If offered a preordered meal, Lynn dissects the menu selection and eats only the parts that fit into her conscious eating routine. Even if you're eating pre-prepared foods or at a restaurant, you can still make more healthful selections or modify the food you're given. Many restaurants post their menus online so you can read them and plan your meals in advance.

Changing your eating habits takes discipline. Aisha Moore, who shared her Self-Care Bill of Rights, asks herself every time she is tempted to order fried foods, "Does this serve my health?" Pay attention to what you are putting into your mouth, pause, and make a conscious decision to cut out the bad and take in more good. Moderation is easier to incorporate into your life than cold turkey abstinence. Slowing down and paying attention to how fast you are eating is a self-care technique. Chew slowly, breathe between bites, put your fork or spoon down, and savor the flavor of your food.

Don't wait until something drastic happens to you to reexamine your eating habits. Check with a nutritionist to find out the right foods to eat and to guide you on your own appropriate eating routine. Other trusted resources online regarding nutrition and healthy eating include the American Heart Association, Kaiser Permanente, and Mayo Clinic.

Wellness Triad: Exercise

There are many forms of exercise that can suit any fitness level, personality type, and available time. Exercise doesn't have to always be about breaking out into a sweat. Slow stretches can warm up your muscles and get your blood flowing, increasing oxygen to your brain. Here are ways nonprofit professionals are fitting exercise into their busy schedules.

Susan Nesbitt, head of Business Development at Make School, experienced work burnout a few years ago. "I didn't get sick enough to land into a hospital, but working hours and days on end, even sleeping under my desk at the office, took its toll." Exercise and fitness were the medicine that helped her heal and return to work.

"I started running, cycling, and doing yoga. I created the patterns that were integrated into my workday, leaving the office for a run during the lunch hour. It was my self-mandate to become as fit and healthy as possible. I treated it as a life or death situation." She started training for the AIDS/LifeCycle, a 600-mile bike route between Los Angeles and San Francisco, to raise money for a good cause and it is something she now does every year.

"I learned over the years that exercise and fitness are cornerstones of life and work. I'd give up everything, but not my yoga mat and running shoes. The only way I can be the best and show up and give to the world is when I am centered and grounded in physical fitness."

If your work constantly keeps you in your head, doing something physical can shift your brain from one way of processing information, signals, and impulses to another. Movement, stretching, and walking can be beneficial not only for relaxing, but to boost your productivity. Using a different part of your brain can also pull your thinking out of a rut, but to reap the benefits, it has to become part of your daily routine.

Allyson Kapin, a founding partner at Rad Campaign, a digital strategy agency that works with nonprofits, discovered the benefits of exercise as a teen. Exercise is just part of the way she lives her life now. "I work out five days a week, and I fit it in by making it a priority. Even if I end up working long hours, I will grab a late night workout because it's important to me, and it makes me feel good—physically and mentally. I need that time for myself."

Carie Lewis Carlson, director of social media marketing at The Humane Society of the United States, examined how she could fit time in for herself into her existing schedule. When she decided she wanted to lose weight, she joined a gym but never went because she was always too tired at the end of the day.

"I found a window of time between dropping my daughter off at day care and going to work," Lewis Carlson explains. "I already have to leave the house, and I found a gym close to day care. I know what time I have to leave and have to do a little extra prep work the night before to save time in the morning." Lewis Carlson made fitness a priority and found a pocket of time to fit it in and establish a routine.

A regular exercise routine is also high on Gina C. Lynn's priority list. "Running on the local trail is the way I 'release the crazy,' and quite possibly, I come up with my best ideas and best practices for Chamber operations when I step away from my desk and spend time in nature."

Lynn's quick tips for succeeding with a well-rounded well-being practice include:

- Start slowly.
- Make little changes.
- Find something you enjoy because you will be more likely to stick to it.
- Enlist a friend to join you to keep you accountable.

You don't have to run to be exercising. Walking 30 minutes a day can have incredible health benefits. And you can integrate exercise and movement into your workday throughout the day with walking meetings, as we will explain in the next chapter.

Peggy Duvette, director of social at NetSuite, gets her exercise while commuting to work by bicycle. "I find it a powerful meditation practice for my mind as well as for my body. I often catch myself in the morning prioritizing my work as I ride," says Duvette. "If I ride before coming home, I don't feel the necessity to talk about my work and maybe share some of its difficulties during dinner since I was unconsciously processing it on the bike."

Sarah Kinney Wright, training and outreach manager at Women's Health & Family Planning Association of Texas, started a group in her area called Dance Walk! Austin. Dance walking is just what it sounds like: doing dance moves while you walk. Wright has even led a few impromptu dance walking groups at her nonprofit.

"I can tell you from direct personal experience with the specific stressors of nonprofit work that dance walking is a fantastic way to burn off the stress that is difficult to shake loose. Dance walking taps into that kid in you that just wants to jump around and do what you want with no boundaries and no rules. Feel the music and go wild or don't." Wright says if you are walking alone, bring your music player and headset and pick songs that pump you up. Pick a location where you're comfortable and feel safe.

These are just a few ways to incorporate exercise into your busy life as part of your self-care. Start with baby steps. Even just getting off the subway or bus several stops early and walking the rest of way to work can get you moving. If you are planning on starting a new exercise routine and are out of shape or have health problems, consult with your doctor to ensure you are doing it in a safe way.

SUPPORTING HAPPINESS AND WELL-BEING

Sometimes, your quest for well-being through self-care is hampered by your mind and the mental interference from bad habits that are ingrained in your routine. The Wellness Triad we just discussed—better sleep, nutrition, and exercise—can affect how your brain works, including the way you process information, focus, and handle stress. There are many other ways to support your overall well-being. Let's start with being mindful.

Mindfulness

A clinical definition of mindfulness is: *"Attending to ongoing events and experiences in a receptive and nonjudgmental way."* You can train your brain to pay more attention, to be aware, and be more attentive through mindfulness practices. Some benefits of mindfulness—regardless of the techniques you use to be more mindful—include:

- Regulating your moods
- Reducing emotional exhaustion
- Increasing your job satisfaction

How effective is mindfulness? A 2014 study showed employees who simply took online courses in mindfulness were less stressed, more resilient, and more energetic.[3] Clearly, those benefits could be useful in all aspects of life, not just work.

There are many ways to be more mindful. Meditation is often the first thing that comes to people's minds. To be clear: mindfulness is not meditation. But if you were to meditate, you'd be stretching and training your mindfulness muscles. A simple way to get started with training your attention is the following exercise:

1. Bring gentle and consistent attention to your breath for two minutes. Every time your attention wanders, bring it back.
2. Sit without an agenda for two minutes. Shift from doing to being.
3. Shift between the two methods for two minutes.

The above practice gets you to the essence of mindfulness. If you practice it enough, it deepens the calm and clarity of your mind. Use this technique when you are overwhelmed at home or work.

Sara Beesley, center director at Mitchell Lake Audubon Center, meditates in the morning before heading off to work. "As my coffee brews, I sit down and clear my brain. I don't know if everyone else's brain is always mentally adding and reordering things on the to-do list, but mine rarely stops. So now I take four minutes and stop. I listen to and smell the coffee brewing and just breathe." This mini-mindfulness moment also helps Beesley later in the day to be more focused at work, tackling her never ending to-do list.

"Long-term, contemplative practices could help reduce anxiety, enhance creativity, improve attention and memory, help you become less reactive in situations with people, and when practiced in groups, can help lead to greater understanding of people from diverse backgrounds and belief systems," says Sharon Parkinson, senior analyst of prospect development and research at Vassar College, who led a workshop on contemplative practices at the college. Parkinson also engages in other forms of contemplative practice like storytelling, prayer, singing, playing music, dancing, working, and volunteering. "Overall, people report just feeling much better emotionally and physically compared to when they began [the practices]."

According to a growing body of research, taking nature walks can soothe your mind and improve your mood, something that Danielle

Brigida, national social media manager at U.S. Fish and Wildlife Service, knows firsthand. Hiking, trail running, and birding are hobbies that help keep her focused and inspired for her work. Taking part in activities in nature also helps her foster friendships with people who value wildlife.

"Any weekend that I make time to explore the outdoors leaves me feeling ready to tackle the week with a healthy bit of optimism. I find that spending time uncovering the natural world, flipping over logs, or watching a bird, helps bring perspective to my day job," says Brigida.

Reflective practice—taking time to sit quietly and reflect on a meeting, an encounter with a coworker, or other occurrence during your day—gives you the time to process a situation to keep stress at bay. For further help with taking mindful minutes, meditating, or to learn longer mindful exercises, check out the list of guided meditation apps at www.happyhealthynonprofit.org. A trusted source of meditation for well-being is the website for the Center for Mindfulness in Medicine, Health Care, and Society at the University of Massachusetts Medical School.

Gratitude

Another way to change your brain and how you perceive your environment and others around you is to engage in gratitude activities. Amber Hacker, alumni relations manager at Interfaith Youth Core, admits she rolled her eyes when she first heard about keeping a gratitude journal. She soon became convinced of its benefits.

"Writing a gratitude journal is a good personal exercise. It has been transformative for me personally," says Hacker. "Every day, I write down three things I'm thankful for. I've started noticing more things to be thankful for."

Studies show that some of the benefits of gratitude include better sleep, higher self-esteem, increased empathy, and more resilience. Even the U.S. Surgeon General, Vivek Murthy, advocates happiness as one way to prevent disease and live a longer, healthier life. Some experts recommend spending five minutes a day identifying the things you are grateful for and feeling gratitude.

And don't keep your gratitude to yourself! Let people around you know you are grateful for them and why. They'll get a boost from the sincere compliment, but so will you from the act of complimenting. You can also use a gratitude app to help you express your gratitude.

Nataly Kogan is the creator of an app called Happier that lets you post things you're grateful for and share them with friends on the app or more widely through Facebook and Twitter. She also offers online courses in happiness through the app, including a five-minute Happiness Workout™, to help people practice these three foundational skills to be happier:

1. Gratitude: Like Amber Hacker, Kogan extols the benefits of writing down three things you're grateful for. "They should be specific and new every day for your brain to register them," says Kogan. "Gratitude has been shown to be the number one predictor of someone's well-being."
2. Kindness: "Do or plan a small act of kindness toward someone in your life every day. Intentional kindness is one of the simplest and most meaningful ways you can become happier."
3. Awareness and Acceptance: Going back to mindfulness, Kogan recommends spending "a few minutes being still and quiet—a short meditation practice to help you become more aware of how you feel." Kogan explains that practicing awareness and acceptance of how you feel helps you make better decisions about what to do in different situations in your life to "live from a place of inner peace versus struggle."

"Happiness isn't the outcome; it's the foundation of living a healthier, more fulfilling life," says Kogan. In addition to her Happier app, we list several other gratitude apps online at www.happyhealthynonprofit.org.

Relaxation

Relaxation and work may seem to be contradictions, particularly when you have a stressful job or work in a toxic environment. But relaxation shouldn't be looked at as something to achieve separate from your work or the workplace. Instead of training your mind and body to relax only when you've distanced yourself from your work, start applying relaxation techniques at work, right in the office, to shift your negative Pavlovian response to work stress. Instead of creating a fight or flight response to stressors around you, integrate relaxation and calm into the place where you work and the way that you work.

We go back to paying attention to your breathing. When stressed, you end up breathing in a more shallow and irregular fashion. The simple act of breathing deeply can bring more oxygen to your brain that, in turn, provides the fuel it needs to function more effectively. Refer to the simple breathing exercise in the earlier section in this chapter on mindfulness. You can even use an app or wearable tech to monitor your stress levels by tracking the way you breathe.

Beth uses the Spire, a wearable device created by the Calming Technology Lab at Stanford University. The Spire device, like a small stone attached to your waistband or bra, streams data to an app, reporting whether you are calm, tense, or focused based on the length, depth, and spacing of your breath. Having data about how many minutes and exactly when you are calm and focused can be useful—especially when you reflect on what activity or environment you were in when it occurred. With this information, you can be more intentional about being calm and focused, particularly when you go into more stressful places and situations.

Other ways to relax at home and at the office include:

- Eliminating clutter. Less mess around you can help reduce stress and anxiety. Two life-changing books about clearing clutter are: *The Life-Changing Magic of Tidying Up: The Japanese Art of Decluttering and Organizing* and *Spark Joy: The Illustrated Guide to The Life-Changing Magic of Tidying Up*, both by Marie Kondo.
- Turning off notifications. Whether calendar reminders and e-mail pings are constantly opening up on your computer or dinging on your phone, too many notifications and reminders can produce anxiety each time they pop up or make a sound. Reduce your notifications to the most important. We'll give you additional tips on tech wellness in Chapter 5.
- Playing music. Even if you need to wear headphones or ear buds, soothing music can help you relax anytime, including in the office. Sometimes, simply the act of wearing headphones—with or without music—can block out noises and distractions, giving you a quiet work environment and sense of calm.

While it might seem counterintuitive, sometimes a certain type of noise can be relaxing. The wrong kind of noise or too many distracting sounds, particularly around the office, can cause a release of excess cortisol, negatively affecting brain function. But experimenting with specific kinds of ambient sound can help you identify the background noise that helps you concentrate better. Apps like Noisli, with atmospheric nature sounds like rain, and Coffitivity, which plays sounds you might hear if you were working from a café, could help you relax, even at the office. Who would have thought noise could be relaxing? Check out the various relaxation and ambient sound-generating apps listed online at www.happyhealthynonprofit.org.

Creativity

A more relaxed mind can help you be more productive and also more creative. In the reverse, being creative can help reduce stress and stimulate your brain to be more productive. The act of being creative activates different parts of your brain, something proven by scientists through the use of brain scans.

Susan Nesbitt from Make School says, "I wasn't as creatively alive as I wanted to be because I just didn't give myself permission. I started drawing, and I find that it lights up my brain in different ways, and it helps me focus. Rather than being a passive consumer of entertainment, creating something by sketching has had enormous benefits."

A popular trend for meditative creativity is the use of adult coloring books specifically designed for grown-ups versus kids. While adult coloring books have been around for a few years, their popularity soared during the holiday season of 2015 when they were among the top-selling books on Amazon. According to clinical psychologist Scott M. Bea, PsyD, adult coloring books can provide pleasure and help our brain relax.

Explains Bea, "Adult coloring requires modest attention focused outside of self-awareness. It is a simple activity that takes us outside ourselves."[4]

Eve Simon, creative director at Beaconfire RED, a digital marketing and web design agency for social good, is an adult coloring book convert. She learned about them on a Facebook post about Johanna Basford's *Enchanted Forest* coloring book.

"As a designer, I love scribbling, so the idea of just grabbing some pens and a coloring book in my free time sounded really appealing. The book was so popular that it was back-ordered on Amazon, so I bought a basic pattern one and some gel pens and instantly fell in love. I think I spent that whole weekend coloring," says Simon.

Simon confesses she is not a "meditation person," but coloring is close to that for her:

> I love that you can focus on just one element at a time, sometimes even just a segment of the drawing. There are times that I just say "let's do leaves for a while" and nothing else in the world matters but them. Sure, I want the whole finished image to look good, but I find it liberating to just go with the flow. Coloring lets me take a break from all the other pressures in my life for a short while and create something beautiful in the process.

Before you think coloring books have no place in a professional workplace, ArtPride NJ used coloring books and crayons as branded promotional giveaways at its Art Matters booth at the New Jersey League of Municipalities conference. "They were a huge hit," says Anne Marie Miller, director of advocacy & public policy at ArtPride NJ. At an annual NTEN Nonprofit Technology Conference, we noted that at least four different booths at the expo attracted attention giving away adult coloring pages and colored pencils.

"I am loving adult coloring books and bought them for my friends who work in the nonprofit field for Christmas. It's such an exercise in mindfulness," says Susie Bowie, president and executive director at Manatee Community. "The act of moving a colored pencil or pen across the paper, without worry about whether I am producing a masterpiece creation, is calming in itself. Meditative in the midst of so much busy."

We are both fans of coloring books, and we are also obsessed with pens and markers. Coloring and drawing brings us back to our childhood love of making art, something Aliza described in the introduction of this book. This kind of association can be comforting while stimulating creativity.

Another type of meditative drawing is called Zentangle, a miniature abstract work of art consisting of a collection of patterns created by Rick Roberts and Maria Thomas. Zentangles are drawn on a small piece of a paper called a "tile" so it can be completed in a short time. The process uses pens and pencils or you can add color with markers. Creating a Zentangle is unplanned, and there are no mistakes, making this art form more relaxing than you might think. We both have used the Zentangle drawing method to take a break from staring at screens and find that it helps with relaxation, focus, and concentration. You can learn more about Zentangles and other similar meditative art forms from books, websites, and apps, some of which we've listed online at www.happyhealthynonprofit.org.

Blogger and nonprofit tech consultant Shai Coggins turns to creative activities like sketching and painting. "Personally, I've always loved art even though I didn't consider myself as an artist when I was younger. I highly encourage adding some kind of creative practice into everyone's self-care regime. Or, at least, make sure to find ways to be surrounded by art. After all, according to research, the brain feels rewarded even just by looking at art."

In addition to making art, Coggins journals. "Journaling isn't just a way to record my day-to-day life or express myself. It also became my way of thinking out loud, brainstorming, and problem-solving. I fell in love with journaling and never stopped. It remains a vital part of my professional and personal life."

After experiencing tremendous benefits from journaling, Coggins published *Today: Life: A Guided Journal on Everyday Moments*.[5] Because journaling is known to have several health and psychological benefits, Coggins wanted to come up with something that can help even the most reluctant journal-keepers record their memories, ideas, and other relevant matters. The guided journal includes prompts and tips to help get you writing immediately along with pages where you can write or doodle anything.

Researchers have found that doing different crafting activities can have a variety of health benefits.[6] Peggy Duvette, who we mentioned earlier, uses knitting to help her relax.

"I got back into knitting around eight years ago as a personal commitment to hand make most of my Christmas presents for my family. While at first it was a decision led by my environmental practice and my desire to reduce consumption, I realized it has become a creative outlet and helped with stress relief," says Duvette. Knitting is not just a woman's hobby. Duvette told us that one of the men on her former organization's board was also a knitter.

We've just presented a variety of ideas for incorporating self-care into your daily life. Any of these techniques can help set the stage for a less-stressed day at work. Next, we will focus on ways you can bring self-care directly into your workplace.

CHAPTER 5

The Workflow

Changing the Way You Work

I found the "notifications off" setting.

BRINGING IT TO THE OFFICE

Because more than one-third of our lives are spent at work, our workplace and how we work are often blamed for causing many of our stresses and woes. An ideal work situation is one where your organization is attentive to the well-being of all staff and stakeholders. A bad working environment is one where stress and turnover are high and morale and energy are low. If you are doing good work in a bad environment and leaving isn't an immediate option for you, you can still make efforts to inoculate yourself against the contagion of chronic stress with your self-care regimen.

Your workplace encompasses all Five Spheres of Happy Healthy Living. We just covered self in the previous chapter. Now we'll look at others, environment, work, and technology, all areas where you can practice self-care. Bringing self-care into your place of work is critical for sustaining your optimum energy levels and helping stave off stress and burnout.

RELATIONSHIPS IN THE WORKPLACE

Your relationships with your coworkers, your boss, your board, and other organization stakeholders can either help you combat stress or can cause it. Stressful work relationships can affect the quality of your time at work and the quality of your work and even your relationships at home. Caring for the relationships you have with others, including your coworkers, attends to your self-care and well-being.

One way to manage the stress that can stem from your relationships in the workplace is to get skilled in emotional intelligence (EI). Daniel Goleman, in his book titled *Emotional Intelligence*, defined EI as the ability to manage yourself and your relationships with others through greater self-awareness and being socially aware or being able to recognize and understand the moods of others.[1] Knowing who and what pushes your buttons at work and managing your own reactions to others is important.

Goleman writes about the specific areas of being socially aware on his website:[2]

- Empathy: Sensing others' feelings and perspectives, and taking an active interest in their concerns
- Organizational awareness: Reading a group's emotional currents and power relationships
- Service orientation: Anticipating, recognizing, and meeting customers' needs

How do you apply social awareness in your workplace? Here are a few tips:

- Ask empowering questions that inspire others.
- Pay attention to what others say, how they say it, and the body language they use.
- Identify other people's emotional states when you are interacting with them.
- Give your full attention when speaking with someone.

Emotional intelligence is helpful in all of your dealings with other people and can be especially useful at a nonprofit. Kaitlyn Jankowski, product marketing manager at charity: water, admits that working in a nonprofit can be hard, especially when it comes to people's emotions.

"I think emotions are high as the organization, and the people that fill it, view their jobs as more than just a job," says Jankowski. "I'm constantly thinking about how each day we, as an organization, are bringing more than 2,700 people clean water. With that being said, it's important to find a way to show empathy, compassion, and kindness in the workplace and also have the ability to decouple that from getting the job done."

Jankowski says she took a leadership development training led by Beth that included emotional intelligence skills training and learned how to keep her emotions in check when she finds they are "doing the talking."

"Over the years I've learned that my physical well-being is directly tied to how I feel in the workplace," Jankowski explains. She says she keeps an eye on when her emotions are running high, remembering to take some deep breaths or walk away. Adds Jankowski, "If I've learned anything, it's that being emotional about your job isn't always a bad thing, but not being able to control those emotions can be detrimental to getting the job done."

Compassion

Being socially aware of other people's emotions can be much more powerful if you also use compassion as you relate to another person. Yes, we're talking about compassion at work. Scientists at Stanford University actually hold a conference called "Compassion and Business," and one of the themes of their 2013 conference was that caring about your own well-being and caring for the well-being of others was not in conflict. So how do you show compassion at work?

Creating happier, healthier relationships with your coworkers involves active listening, showing respect, and being kind. Start with common courtesy such as avoiding negative behaviors toward others or using negative words about others in the workplace. Don't join in when the gossip mill is churning. Instead, celebrate the wins of your team members by shining a light on those who deserve the kudos. Never take claim for someone else's work. Avoid negativity by not creating it or contributing to it.

If you're in a work environment where you or others are suffering from or at the risk of succumbing to compassion fatigue, deliberately bring more compassion into the workplace for one another to help offset this kind of stress. A card or handwritten note of encouragement can do wonders. Giving someone else your full attention is compassionate. Thanking someone for even the smallest positive actions can have a major impact on how others respond to you and also on how you feel.

Boundaries

Being compassionate can work wonders for a coworker relationship, but there are times when you have to stand firm and protect yourself as a part of your self-care. An effective skill to better manage your multifaceted life is to set boundaries. Boundary setting at work tends to fall by the wayside when we worry our job may be in jeopardy if we say no to requests, particularly from managers.

Setting boundaries in small ways can give you the time and space you need to keep stress at bay without offending anyone. The Social Transformation Project offers a suite of assessments tools around "personal ecology" to "create balance, pacing, and efficiency to support a lifetime of sustained service." You can download free articles and assessment tools to understand where you are not keeping good boundaries and how you can apply different techniques for greater balance.

Wendy Harman, formerly the director of Information Management and Situational Awareness at the Red Cross and now a White House Presidential Innovation Fellow, uses an accountability buddy technique around boundaries.

"A friend of mine and I have a list of daily questions we ask ourselves, and we spend about 10 minutes on the phone with each other once a week," says Harman. "Some weeks we're way overboard on work and others we're oversubscribed in our personal lives, but we ensure we're balanced overall and on track."

To get into the habit of setting healthier boundaries, practice saying "no." Saying no may feel uncomfortable, but doing so allows you to establish boundaries, keep expectations of others in check, and keep your workload more focused and relevant to your roles and responsibilities. Here's a simple four-step path to saying no:

1. Set intentional priorities. Clearly establish and write down the things that are important to you that require your time, attention, presence, and effort.
2. Weigh requests against your current workload and home life responsibilities plus your long-term goals. Be honest with yourself.
3. Evaluate the time, resources, and attention it will take if you say yes to each request. What will it take away from the things you've established are important to you?
4. Just say no.

For more reasons to say no, check out Derek Sivers' video and writings about the "Hell Yeah" at https://sivers.org/hellyeah. If those don't motivate you to say no and draw your boundary lines, we don't know what will! Boundary setting at work can help reduce some of your stress, but look around you: your office environment could also be stressing you out.

ENVIRONMENT

Your environmental self-care efforts at work can start in small but obvious ways such as making physical changes in your cubicle or around your office space. There are many techniques for modifying your physical space, including the ancient and often-practiced methods of feng shui, and the contemporary methods of Marie Kondo. Let's look at both to see which technique might suit your personality and your physical work environment.

Feng shui is an ancient Chinese system of arranging both indoor and outdoor spaces to encourage the flow of positive energy or *qi* (pronounced "chee"). You can design buildings for "auspicious" or optimal and advantageous placement and positioning for good energy flow. A few common feng shui techniques include placing your desk in a "power position" so you are facing into the room and not with your back to the door; you should be able to see all windows and entryways in front of you. Not being able to see who is approaching you as you sit at your desk is disruptive to your energy. If you cannot arrange your desk in this manner, place a small mirror on the wall in front of you so you can see when someone is behind you. Position plants at the corners of your desk to soften the sharp edges of your desk corners. Sharp edges disrupt the smooth flow of *qi*.

Choose colors such as off-white and pale shades that are pleasing to the eye. Display artwork in your office that reflects the state of mind you want to both project and absorb—calm, clear, and prosperous, for example. Try to represent all five natural elements in your office: wood, earth, metal, water, and fire. Look to balance out your space; if you have too much metal, bring in something made of wood. If you have too many angles, bring in something round or with curves. Keep office accessories simple and orderly.

Clearing clutter is a major aspect of feng shui. A modern version of tidying spaces is introduced in two books by *New York Times* best-selling author and professional organizer, Marie Kondo: *The Life-Changing Magic of Tidying Up: The Japanese Art of Decluttering and Organizing*[3] and *Spark Joy: An Illustrated Master Class on the Art of Organizing and Tidying Up*.[4] Kondo's process involves examining why you are holding on to an item and literally holding it and asking yourself, "Does it spark joy?" If not, give it away or throw it out. Once you have eliminated clutter, you will gain a new perspective, more energy, and more clarity. Kondo suggests you do this for every room in your house starting with your closet and clothes and moving to all objects. You can also apply these techniques to your office.

Setting a more pleasing ambience does not have to be complicated. Holistic health coach Rochelle Ludovisi suggests using aromatherapy to reduce stress and produce an environment that is pleasant and calming. Look for high-quality essential oils that appeal to you, and bring them to the office. Note any coworkers who might be allergic to certain scents. If you are restricted from using an aromatherapy diffuser in the office, keep a bottle in your bag and pull it out periodically to inhale a scent such as vanilla or lavender for relaxation, or peppermint or orange to energize. Consult an aromatherapist to find your ideal scents.

Ludovisi also recommends bringing a Himalayan salt lamp into your office to help purify the air. The soft light can turn any room into a more relaxing space with just the flip of a switch. Use an ionic air purifier to remove pollen and dust particles from the air. We don't always pay attention to our sense of smell, but clearing the air in our offices and training our brains to associate certain scents with relaxation can give us a lift and a boost against stress.

Physical cues are important for triggering positive behaviors. Temptation goes both ways. You can be tempted by packaged cookies, chips, and candy bars, or you can put healthier options within reach and be tempted by those. If storing your healthy snacks in the office break room or fridge isn't a viable option, consider getting a small cube fridge to have near your workstation, and stock it with yogurt, fresh fruits and vegetables, nuts, and water. What about putting a fruit basket with fresh fruit on your desk by your computer next to a plant?

Clearing your work environment and the energy in your workspace can take you only so far. You also need to learn to manage your personal energy and workflow. Believe it or not, how and when you work may not be optimal for the way your body and brain are genetically structured to operate.

YOUR WORKFLOWS

A work process filled with interruptions is not good for your workflow and can impair your productivity. A brain that drifts away from attention isn't at its best. If you find yourself getting distracted often, try Peter Bregman's "18 Minutes a Day" technique from his book of the same name.[5] It is two 5-minute periods and then 1 minute for each of the 8 hours of a typical workshop day which equals 18 minutes. Here's how it works:

- For five minutes in the morning, think of and write down three important things you want to accomplish that day.
- Set your smartphone to beep every hour and when it does, spend 1 minute asking yourself if you are on track. Do this 8 times for an average 8-hour workday.
- For five minutes at the end of the day, ask yourself, "What did I accomplish? What didn't I accomplish? Why?"

You might think the hourly beeps would be distracting, but they are reminders to stay focused. An exercise like this can help you manage your attention. With better attention comes better focus and energy. Janet Fouts, social media consultant and author of *Mindful Social Media*, suggests asking yourself throughout the day, "What am I doing?" and "Is this important?"

Says Fouts, "Lots of times you can catch yourself procrastinating by doing anything but the one thing you need to be doing. A little practice can shorten that wasted time."

If you find yourself choosing to work on undemanding, low priority tasks instead of important work priorities, procrastination may be an issue for you and an early warning sign of burnout. You need to be more aware of when, why, and how you are procrastinating. Boredom, fear, distaste, being ill equipped, overloaded, or overwhelmed are some triggers for avoiding a particular work task.

How can you avoid procrastination? Best-selling self-help book author Brian Tracy says in his book, *Eat That Frog*, "If the first thing you do each morning is to eat a live frog, you can go through the rest of the day with the satisfaction of knowing that that is probably the worst thing that is going to happen to you all day long."[6]

He's not literally saying to eat a frog, of course! Your "frog" is your biggest, most important task, the one that you are most likely to put off if you don't do something about it. So eat that frog early, and get the added benefit of making a positive impact on your day.

Is your procrastination due to being overwhelmed? If so, try making a "not-to-do list," says Vu Le of Rainier Valley Corps. A not-to-do list can be an antidote to the never-ending to-do list or as Beth calls it, a "no thank-you list."

Le explains, "It can be a list of stuff you are currently doing that you might want to consider no longer doing. For example, do you really need to have a staff meeting every week or is biweekly okay? It can also be a list of stuff that you are currently not doing, but it'll make you feel better to write them down and check them off."

Le may be half-joking with his suggestion, however, sometimes we need to shake things up to be able to push through the times when we have less focus or low energy for our work.

MANAGING YOUR ENERGY

Most of us think that the secret sauce to productivity is time management, but energy management is just as important. We've talked about circadian rhythms, your natural cycles of wake and sleep based on light and dark. As with other living things, your energy is like the ocean, with a high tide of peak attention and energy and a low tide of difficulty concentrating and needing to rest. It's time to get to know your *ultradian rhythms*, another type of natural rhythm that repeats throughout the day.

"I take breaks to stretch my eyes and body every 90 to 120 minutes," says Fission Strategy CEO Cheryl Contee, who applies techniques to work with, not against, her ultradian rhythms. "I got this tip from a great book I highly recommend: *The Way We're Working Isn't Working* by Tony Schwartz.[7] I was actually at an airport gate area hunched over, working my laptop, iPad, and iPhone simultaneously, and looked up to see an ad for the book. It hit a nerve!"

In his book, Schwartz explains that our brains can only focus for 90 to 120 minutes before they need a break for 10 to 20 minutes. An effective way to manage your energy is to sync your work routine to your ultradian rhythms, designing your workday based around them. Realistically, you cannot have complete control of your daily calendar, especially within an organization where your time is not always your own. But be aware of your energy flows and try to plan out your work tasks to align with these cycles. Once you start working with, not against, your energy, you'll find that you're more productive.

Movement as Work

Another way to manage your energy at work is to address the fact that you are definitely sitting at your desk too much during your workday. Get into the practice of moving around by taking stretch breaks to refresh your mind and rejuvenate your muscles. You may also want to try standing more often at work.

One way to stand more but stay productive is to use a standing desk that serves as both a visual cue and a physical change to your office environment. A standing desk can transform the way you work and the energy you have for work. It also helps to address the negative toll sitting has on your body.

Full standing desks can be expensive, but you can buy standing desk adapters that sit on a regular desk or hack a standing desk with boxes, books, or other techniques to prop up your computer and keyboard at the optimum levels. Ask for a standing desk in the office that you can share with your coworkers. Then prompt each other to take turns standing throughout the day. Involving some of your coworkers in your self-care journey can be enlightening and motivating for you and for them.

As you begin standing more often, invest in a soft pad for your feet as they may get sore while you get used to standing at your desk. Also check that your standing desk is set up ergonomically correct to avoid injury. As with any habit change, start with short periods of standing and then sit for a while until you build up the stamina to stand for longer periods. Or follow the 20/8/2 Rule from ergonomic expert Alan Hedges: 20 minutes sitting, 8 minutes standing, and 2 minutes stretching.[8]

Now that we have you out of your chair, don't just stand there. Start walking! Walking can do wonders for your self-care, and you can integrate it as part of your work. Walking at work is a powerful antidote to stress. As we mentioned in the introduction, Beth changed her sedentary habits by strapping on a Fitbit and incrementally increasing her daily steps from 2,000 to 15,000 or more. Here are some of Beth's tips for changing the way you think about—and do—walking:

- Stop thinking of solo walking as exercise. Walking is a great time to think about challenging work tasks.
- Recognize when you are not productive sitting and take a five-minute walk around your office. Stretch.
- Incorporate 20- to 30-minute solo walks during the day or walk and take care of calls at the same time on your mobile phone.
- Start a walking commute to work, if possible, or park further away from your office or get off the bus a stop early so you can walk to start your day.

Beth is a big advocate of walking *as* work. Walking as work isn't a new idea. Aristotle was said to walk as he taught and founded what is now called the Peripatetic school of philosophy. Peripatetic refers to "traveling, wandering, walking, and meandering." See Chapter 8 for details on how to hold walking meetings.

Even if you aren't stepping away from your desk to walk, you can still add movement to your day. We mentioned stretch breaks earlier when talking about ultradian rhythms, but regular stretching can also help you avoid what Jacqui Burge, founder of Desk Yogi, calls "numb butt."

"When I sat for more than four hours a day, I would actually lose feeling in my butt and down my legs," explains Burge. "That's why I invested in a standing desk, but then my legs hurt because I still needed to move my body."

Burge created Desk Yogi, an app for your computer that reminds you to pause and stretch and guides you through easy yoga moves, breathing exercises, and stretches right at your desk. Any movement tied to breath is beneficial, Burge explains.

The key to integrating stretching and desk yoga into your routine is to not only set up alerts on your phone or computer prompting you to stretch but to make sure you don't ignore them.

Having a simple routine you can follow is also important. Burge recommends changing up your stretch routines to avoid becoming bored and losing interest. While it may seem awkward at first to stretch or do yoga at your desk, especially in an open office, your coworkers will notice the benefits you receive and get inspired. The beauty of desk yoga is it can be done anytime, rain or shine.

Another option for integrating more movement at work is to use a treadmill desk. Author and consultant Kivi Leroux Miller noticed a pattern when tracking her movement: when the weather was bad, she accumulated fewer steps.

Says Leroux Miller, "I decided getting a treadmill desk was the best option. Even on busy days, I can usually walk 30 to 60 minutes on the treadmill, and I can't use weather as an excuse."

Leroux Miller experimented to figure out which work tasks she could accomplish on the treadmill desk. "I need to do a lot of reading of paper books and reading online, and that's perfect for walking on the treadmill—same with watching videos. I can also do a fair amount of brainstorming and mind mapping, which I do with pen and paper on the treadmill."

She warns that some tasks, such as anything requiring precise mouse movements, are impossible on a treadmill desk and that typing can be a challenge. She tags her to-do list with "treadmill" for those tasks she knows she can accomplish on the treadmill. "When I'm ready to walk, I just see what I tagged," she says.

Standing desks, treadmill desks, desk yoga, walking, and even simply stretching can improve both your posture and productivity while also helping to reduce your stress. Remember to check out Chapter 8 for an introduction to walking meetings. We're not kidding!

ASKING FOR FLEXIBLE WORK

We've talked about workflow and movement as well as energy management and how typical work schedules and routines may not coincide with your optimal work times. Think about the changes you can make to your daily routine that will help keep your energy up so you work more efficiently. You could immediately improve the quality of your work and day through flexible work structures and schedules.

Carie Lewis Carlson of The Humane Society, introduced in Chapter 4, says having a child really opened her eyes to the need for self-care. Lewis Carlson was motivated to ask for flextime when she found that working until 9:00 P.M. meant her daughter would always be in bed by the time she got home.

"When I came back from maternity leave, my life had changed completely. I went from work being my one and only priority to being a working mom overnight," Lewis Carlson recalls. "I had a really hard time adjusting to this, so I decided to ask my manager for a meeting. I was honest in telling her I was struggling to get some balance and asked if she would be open to trying a part-time work-from-home arrangement. And, I told her that if it didn't work, for any reason—like she didn't feel like she could communicate well enough with me, my direct reports needed more supervision, etcetera—that this was only a month-long trial."

Now Lewis Carlson works from home two days a week. She also leaves the office by 5:00 P.M. every day without apology. Lewis Carlson makes it a point to communicate with her supervisor about what she needs in terms of work flexibility. From there, they work out what is best for her and what works for the organization. Her advice to others seeking flextime is to be ready with a solution—or several scenarios—that would meet your needs and the needs of the organization. Start with a trial period to test the waters.

Rachel Calderon, marketing and communications manager at Central Florida Foundation, asked for a flex schedule when she returned to work after having her second child. Calderon leaves work early two days a week with the agreement to stay connected through e-mail, available for phone calls, and remote access from home.

"I also have a lot of flexibility to work from home if I have a sick child or something going on at home. This allows me to beat traffic on the way home, spend some extra time with my kids, start dinner, and do a few things around the house. The extra time really helps with the work-life balance and helping me feel like I'm ahead," says Calderon, who adds that her organization benefits from allowing her to work flexibly because it gets the "best version" of her.

Flextime is not an official employment policy at Calderon's organization. Before she went out on maternity leave, she had several conversations with her boss about what she needed to be able to come back to work and be okay. Her supervisor took the proposal up with the organization's CEO who agreed as long as Calderon's time in and out of the office was consistent so that the other staff would know what to expect. Calderon wrote a formal memo, and she and her supervisor review her schedule every 90 days to make sure it still works for everyone.

Megan Keane, who works at NTEN and is a part-time yoga teacher, asked for schedule flexibility so she could continue teaching. Says Keane, "It is very helpful to teach a yoga class as a complement to the day job as it flexes a different part of my brain. The benefit is that I'm more focused at work."

Ash Shepherd, one of Keane's coworkers at NTEN, is the parent of young children. He requested multiple accommodations in his schedule to align with his children's school schedules, working at home for a few weeks at a time instead of going into the office or scheduling his own "bring your kids to work" days as needed.

For Shepherd, this flexibility allows him to balance the needs of work and his children without feeling the full brunt of stress. Says Shepherd, "This benefits NTEN because it allows me to bring my best, in whatever form the schedule needs to look like. If I was constantly feeling the pressure of my needs in my personal life and professional life, I would hit a point of burnout very quickly, become less productive, and likely feel like I needed a new job in order to find balance." Shepherd admits he felt the latter in a previous job.

Here are tips from Shepherd for requesting to work remotely and balancing parenting with maximum productivity:

- Be honest with yourself. When you need to take the day off if you have sick child, acknowledge that you won't be productive working from home.
- Stay in touch. Good communications with your team when you are working remotely is essential. Make a conscious effort to reach out

via e-mail or instant messaging so your colleagues know you are being productive.

- Know yourself. If you don't have the discipline to get things done working remotely, don't set yourself up for failure.
- Establish a routine. When working remotely, don't forget to take breaks if you get too absorbed in your work.
- Keep work-at-home space separate from personal space. Working at your kitchen table may not be best for your productivity. Find a separate space in the house, if possible.

Bottom line is if you do not ask for what you need, you definitely will not get it. Your self-care often requires planning and proposing to get others on board with you. If you ask for flexible work and present a clear plan for how that will benefit your organization, you have a good chance of getting buy-in from your supervisor for a work routine change.

BRINGING PLAY TO YOUR WORK

Now let's shake things up a little more. Let's play! According to HelpGuide.org, a guide for mental health and well-being, "play is not just essential for kids; it can be an important source of relaxation and stimulation for adults as well." Adult play is a time to "forget about work and commitments, and to be social in an unstructured, creative way. The focus of play is on the actual experience, not on accomplishing any goal."

Yes, we are talking about play at the office. Appropriate play, of course. Some other benefits of play include stress relief, improved brain function, increased energy, creativity boosts, and stronger bonds with others. Don't those all sound like valuable tools for working well?

Industrial-organizational psychologist Keris Jän Myrick, MBA, MS, PhDc, and former CEO of Project Return Peer Support Network, says people "can't help people if they aren't in their own wellness zone." In addition to a number of other self-care activities, Myrick uses toys for stress relief, including robots.

"Robots help me get my stress out," Myrick explains and says she uses them to help people make decisions—to "robot it out." She uses kaleidoscopes as a small way to escape, stress balls to squeeze and Play-Doh to play with to relieve tension.

Sheena Greer is a nonprofit writer and strategist, and founder of Colludo—Latin for "play together." She encourages nonprofit professionals to find ways to playfully approach their work, and her company even organizes "play days" for organizations.

Says Greer, "This hard work of saving the world should be fun sometimes, right? But with so many expressing to me that there was no room for play in their worlds, I realized that I needed to do something."

Greer believes play is crucial to a healthy, balanced life and a powerful way to change nonprofit culture. Here are some tips from Greer to get you into play mode:

- Stop thinking of play as a frivolous waste of time. Play is necessary for good personal health, for healthy relationships, and for big change.
- Take time to play with other grown-ups, including coworkers. Try things like playing board games or tag in the park.
- Create a culture of play at your office. Even if you're not the boss, model play behavior to naturally encourage others to join in.

Here are some of our ideas for play at work:

- Distribute small puzzles, games, or toys throughout the office that anyone can pick up at any time to relieve stress.
- Bring a kid's joke book to work (more likely to be work appropriate) and take turns telling jokes before the start of a meeting.
- Take a quick break during a walking meeting (see Chapter 8) to toss a squishy ball around.
- Blow up balloons and have a pile of them in your office or cubicle to bat around solo or with others throughout the day.
- Bring a deck of cards or board games to work and play a game in the break room at lunch.
- Bring a jump rope to jump solo (or invite others to join you) outside during a work break.
- Laugh. The act of laughing can be a brain and body reset, is good for your mental and physical health, and can be contagious.

Says Greer, "Play is disruptive. It shakes up our everyday way of approaching our work, each other, and even ourselves. And in a field where outdated best practices and overwork reign, we could all use an opportunity to play together."[9]

BREAKING FROM WORK

Play may be helpful for relieving work-related stress, but you still need to take other kinds of deliberate breaks throughout your day to avoid burnout. Taking breaks is critical to working at your optimal levels of focus and attention, productivity, and creative thinking as well as coping with stressors. Breaks from work can come in all shapes and sizes and at any time of the workday.

Designate times to physically step away from your work to give your mind a short rest. Where you can, fill those breaks with movement or quiet. Even switching up where you are doing your work can refresh your thinking. Only you can know what types of breaks work best for your body and brain and for your work situation and environment.

Taking Daily Breaks

As we've advised throughout this book, start by making small, incremental changes before tackling the big ones. Incorporate smaller breaks into your workday as an integral part of work. Make breaks scheduled events in your day to give them importance.

Cheryl Contee of Fission Strategy, who works to her ultradian rhythms, learned that taking longer breaks in the late afternoon—power naps, walks, workouts—clears her mind and recharges her batteries.

"It makes a huge difference in my creativity and productivity during the day," Contee says.

For Bobi Rinehart, lead development officer at the University of Alaska Anchorage, taking a break to walk in the middle of her workday is a fairly established routine. In the summers, she brings her dog to the office and walks with her outdoors. In the winters, she walks through indoor breezeways between buildings on campus. Rinehart admits she can't pull herself away from her desk to walk until she is certain she has made a note of pending tasks.

"I can't relax or switch gears if I'm thinking about all the many things I have to do while I'm walking. But walking does help me look at work situations differently, getting me in a different frame of mind," says Rinehart. Knowing what she needs to do to get up from her desk and get moving is key to sticking with her routine.

Breaks are not excuses to avoid doing your work but instead are critical to getting work done and getting it done well. Making self-care a priority means elevating the things that are good for you to the top of your priority list. Take your break time seriously.

Taking Real Vacations

Sometimes, you need a longer break from work. It's called a vacation! Hoarding vacation time and showing it off as a sign of how self-sacrificing and dedicated you are to your organization's mission is short sighted and the antithesis of self-care. Just as you should not hold up your overtime or lack of sleep as a badge of honor and perseverance, do not put credence in the notion that never taking a vacation is admirable in any way. If you cannot honor your need for respite and replenishment, nobody else will.

"There's this weird culture in nonprofits about not taking your vacation time, like you 'shouldn't' or it's 'frowned upon,'" says Lewis Carlson. "I think it's absolutely ridiculous. I work hard. I earned that time, and it's my time to recharge."

To get others on board in honoring your vacation, Lewis Carlson suggests communicating ahead of time to give people a heads up to coordinate with you right away if they anticipate needing something while you're out.

"I send an e-mail to the Communications staff and others I work with about a week ahead of time. We also have a shared Outlook calendar that everyone uses for time out of the office, and there you can put if you're working from home, completely unreachable, or reachable via text, e-mail, IM, etcetera."

When it comes to time off, Lewis Carlson says she disconnects and lets people know that the only way to reach her is through text and only for emergencies. Every now and then, Lewis Carlson admits, someone does not know she is out on vacation and might try to reach her.

"But that's what out-of-office messages are for. I never list my cell phone number in an out-of-office message when I'm on vacation. I have one person listed as a contact in my absence, and that person knows how to get ahold of me in an emergency."

Lewis Carlson says she always feels more energized both personally and professionally when she returns from a trip, even when it is a work-related conference. Vacations are invaluable. If you cannot remember the last time you went on a real vacation, drop this book, and schedule it now!

TECH WELLNESS

We've covered techniques for implementing self-care related to the spheres of self, others, environment, and work. The final sphere where you can practice self-care in the workplace is around technology. With the myriad ways your tech use is affecting your body and brain, it stands to reason that incorporating tech wellness into your self-care plan will alleviate stress and damage to your health and well-being.

Before we go on, we want to reiterate that we love technology. We do not see technology as a culprit. In fact, we advocate using tech gadgets and apps as tools to encourage wellness and well-being including fitness motivators, nutrition trackers, mindfulness reminders, and relaxation devices. We provide a list of apps and wearable tech we recommend at our website, www.happyhealthynonprofit.org.

Tech wellness starts with awareness of how you relate to your tech and how it is affecting you. You need to develop better habits around how you use technology on a daily basis and that includes changing from a mindless use of smartphones and mobile devices to being more in control and mindful. You need to develop what Howard Rheingold[10] calls "infotention skills" or training your attention and developing better productivity habits given all the online information you consume.

Using technology in a thoughtful way is referred to as "conscious computing," a term coined by Alex Soojung-Kim Pang in his book *The Distraction Addiction: Getting the Information You Need and the Communication You Want, Without Enraging Your Family, Annoying Your Colleagues, and Destroying Your Soul.*[11] This classification of technology use is also referred to as "calming technology" or "contemplative computing." We like to refer to certain apps, chosen with care and for specific benefits, as "mindful tech." These apps can transform your mobile phone, tablet, and computer from agents of distraction into agents of mindfulness.

Activities to help you begin a healthier relationship with your technology can start at home but can also be applied at work. Here are a few things that Aliza recommends to stop being tempted by digital devices and reduce the anxiety and stress that come from using them compulsively instead of mindfully:

- Set up a charging station. Put chargers and devices at the entrance to your home and leave them at the door instead of in the kitchen, family room, or bedroom.

- Keep all electronics out of the bedroom. Don't interfere with your circadian rhythms by looking at screens before bedtime.
- Keep all electronics away from the spaces where you are eating. Keep smartphones off the meal table.
- Turn off smartphones and tablets and tuck them away in a bag or leave them in your car when meeting with someone face to face. Don't cheat by putting them on silent or vibrate.

Turning off your phone completely may not be an option because of your work. In that case, remove all nonessential and non-work-related notifications on your phone and turn down the sound. Unless you are on call as part of your job or are responsible for tracking social media for your organization, stop responding to notifications in a Pavlovian way.

Daniel Levitin, author of *The Organized Mind: Thinking Straight in the Age of Information Overload*, says brain science dictates that you should chunk your day into project periods.[12] Designate time for your social networking instead of dipping into it all day long. The same goes for e-mail—"time box" checking and responding to e-mails at designated intervals. Timeboxing means allocating a fixed time period, a time box, to any planned activity. Controlling your interactions with your technology helps you control your interactions with others so you can manage your workload and information intake. Do not let the constant dinging and buzzing of your electronics make you slave to distractions or to work when you are away from work.

Sara Beesley, center director at the Mitchell Lake Audubon Center, stopped using her phone as an alarm clock—a common technique we have mentioned several times already because it is simple, effective, and has helped many people who are seeking tech wellness.

"Every day, the alarm on my phone would go off, and I would reach over, turn it off, and immediately switch over to my e-mail and check the e-mails I missed between going to bed and waking up," says Beesley. "I would end up staying in bed another 30 minutes, answering e-mails via phone because others were already up and working, and I felt I had to appear to be right there with them. After I gave it up, I suddenly had much more free time in the morning and feel calmer." Beesley now gives her mobile phone and e-mail a curfew.

We aren't saying throw out your electronics or to heck with tech. There are ways to use online tools, mobile apps, and software to help lengthen your attention span and replace information overload with a sense of mindfulness and calm. We share a list of mindful tech uses online at www.happyhealthynonprofit.org. Trying all of the tips we've shared at once might be daunting, but a good place to start could be going cold turkey. Let us explain.

Digital Detox

You've probably heard the term "digital detox," a period of time when a person does not use electronic devices, like smartphones or computers, to reduce stress. Eliminating hyperconnectivity and the constant temptation of checking messages and notifications can do your mind and body a lot of good. Going cold turkey from your electronic devices through a digital detox is very effective. You may be surprised at how quickly your relationship with your tech will shift from compulsion to calm.

Another term for digital detox is a digital sabbath, something proposed in The Sabbath Manifesto[13] from a Jewish organization called Reboot, to help people slow down to counter an increasingly hectic world. The manifesto includes 10 principles that can help you wean yourself off your tech devices and fill your weekends with more mindful and soul-enriching activities. The 10 principles are:

1. Avoid technology.
2. Connect with loved ones.
3. Nurture your health.
4. Get outside.
5. Avoid commerce.
6. Light candles.
7. Drink wine.
8. Eat bread.
9. Find silence.
10. Give back.

You do not have to be Jewish to reap the rewards of a tech-free weekend. Reboot also organizes the National Day of Unplugging every year on the first Friday of March. You can sign up on its website, http://nationaldayofunplugging.com, to take the pledge to unplug on that day. Of course, you do not have to wait until next March to try a digital detox and disconnect from your electronics. You can start by simply turning off your smartphone or mobile device in the evenings after work or on the weekends.

David Neff, consultant and author of *The Future of Nonprofits*, uses "screenless Saturdays," where he simply puts his phone away each Saturday. Neff admits it is hard to abstain because he still has to look at his phone for directions, but overall he makes a conscious decision not to look at his e-mail, texts, or "the true devil, Facebook," as he puts it. "Technology breaks, even just for one day, have been great for me and my family," says Neff.

John Kenyon, a nonprofit technology consultant, takes a social media break every year for three weeks in December. "Part of my work life is in social media, and it can be an endless treadmill which becomes exhausting to my attention span and even my empathy. Taking a break is important to help me refocus on what is important in real life." Kenyon is also mindful of where technology "leaks" into his life and intentionally does not have his phone with him at all times.

Presidential Innovation Fellow Wendy Harman has also practiced going phoneless. Says Harman, "Back in 2010, I purposefully looked for havens where I couldn't have my phone. I was reacting to the intensity of the Haiti earthquake response. I remembered kayaking on various vacations and loving it, so I joined the Washington Canoe Club here in D.C. I love being out on the water, and it's become a peaceful ritual I look forward to. Bonus is that my dog Stella often hitches a ride with me out there."

Harman also engages in hobbies during the weekend that take her away from the screen. "I adore gardening and spend lots of hours on the weekends taking care of my little yard and veggie garden." Another way she escapes from the screen is to listen to music.

Susan Tenby, who has worked in the nonprofit technology sector for a number of years, says she uses yoga to get a break from screens. As Tenby spends a good portion of her working day online, being present in her physical body helps her focus.

"When I do handstands, it's all about shifting my weight, and I can't think about anything else like what's going on in my social media feeds," says Tenby.

Start incrementally with your digital detox. Even just using holidays as an opportunity to unplug can put you on the right track. You will come to realize nothing bad usually happens when you're not connected, and you did not miss anything.

Tech wellness, like any self-care practice, requires:

- Your attention (mindfulness)
- Setting boundaries (balance)
- Forming good habits (behavior)
- Eliminating negative influences
- Having a positive attitude

When your relationship with tech is healthier, *you* become healthier. And happier.

We hope the past two chapters sparked some ideas and inspiration toward your personal quest for happy and healthy in your home life and at work. If you engage in even a small number of the activities we covered, you should experience less stress, increased energy, and more motivation to integrate good habits into your days. Now, let's move on to Part II of this book to expand the concept of self-care from individual practice to an organizational culture of well-being.

PART II

Revitalize Your Organization

CHAPTER 6

The Culture

Transforming Your Organization

Come to think of it, kicking off our well-being program with a croissant-cigars-and-cognac social *was* a bad idea.

CONNECTING THE DOTS TO ORGANIZATIONAL CULTURE CHANGE

Organizational culture is hard to define, but we know culture when we see it—or more precisely—when we work in it and feel it every day. Organizational culture is a complex tapestry made up of attitudes, values, behaviors, and artifacts of the people who work for your nonprofit. Culture is an often-unwritten set of norms that influences the way everyone in your nonprofit organization perceives his or her work, behaves at work, and does his or her work.

The CultureLabX, a global community of "future of work" practitioners, defines workplace culture as:[1]

- **Purpose:** Connects daily work to the vision
- **Values:** Beliefs about what's most important
- **Behaviors:** Actions that are guided by values
- **Recognition:** Applauds those who bring company values to life
- **Rituals:** Repeated behaviors that establish a community
- **Cues:** Reminders that keep people in touch with purpose

A nonprofit's culture is the sum of the collective mind-sets and behaviors of all its employees, even the board. Nobody actually wants to engage in behavior that amplifies stress and leads to dysfunction—like working more than 60 hours per week without breaks. But if leadership is doing it, staff feels expected to follow suit, and soon everyone is doing it. Conversely, if a nonprofit's executive director models self-care and views it as mission critical, this outlook becomes the cultural norm throughout the organization.

In the article "Promoting Healthy Workplaces by Building Cultures of Health and Applying Strategic Communications" published in the February 2016 issue of *Journal of Occupational & Environmental Medicine*, the authors wrote: "Key elements that contribute to a culture of health are leadership commitment, social and physical environmental support, and employee involvement."[2] Simply having a wellness or well-being program isn't enough. Workplace wellness guru Laura Putnam puts it this way: "If you don't have a culture that supports wellness and well-being, your program won't get off the ground."

Because workplace culture is one of the key factors determining whether your nonprofit organization can scale a Happy, Healthy Strategy, you first need to assess the environment of your organization. Is your organization's culture one where happy and healthy can thrive? Or is it one where employee self-care is being ignored, or even worse, ridiculed or penalized? If you don't have a workplace environment conducive to wellness and well-being, your organization must change.

Maddie Grant, an expert in workplace culture and founding partner at WorkXO, agrees the first step to implementing a wellness program is to understand and define where your organization is culturally. Says Grant, "It isn't just defining wellness or health as a value in the abstract, it needs to be connected to the organization's values. People in the organization need to believe that wellness is just as good for them as it is for the organization. And, it isn't just an individual being healthy. It has to be part of a community in the workplace that understands the benefits. For example, if you are healthy and happy, you have more energy to collaborate with your team."

Grant suggests that a nonprofit needs to understand the cultural dynamics of its workplace—what it is like to work there. Her company has developed the "Workplace Genome,"[3] a 15-minute survey that is less of an assessment than a way to profile and understand the workplace culture. The survey helps organizations analyze their capacity for collaboration, innovation, agility, and diversity.

Says Grant, "When you are thinking of culture change, don't think of it as fixing things. You need to map out what it is like to work in the organization, and then look at where you want to be. Your strategy or plan, which consists of activities, programs, and initiatives, is how you get from A to B."

Jennifer Edwards, founding partner at Edwards & Skybetter, worked for many years teaching stress management techniques to staff at nonprofits and corporations.

"While the techniques helped, in a way they added to their stress because the employer would say: 'Okay, we brought in a coach for the day, so now you can deal with your stress.' But in reality, the culture didn't change from unrealistic work demands and, in some cases, a culture that did not support wellness," Edwards recalls.

Edwards says she encountered organizational cultures that rewarded unhealthy habits while discouraging healthy ones. For example, if staff said they needed to take a break by having a cigarette, they were allowed to do so. But, if they wanted to do something healthy like meditate to reduce stress, coworkers rolled their eyes or management frowned upon it. To be more effective in her work, she decided to go back to school and get a degree in organizational change management.

Says Edwards, "I wanted to bring these techniques into the workplace without being the 'stress management coach,' and have wellness be part of an overall game plan for the organization. If you only work on the organizational culture, employees don't get the personalized help they need. If individuals work on their stress without having an organizational culture of wellness, it doesn't work either. Both employees and the organization need to understand the benefits and create the space to shift the culture."

Edwards notes that for an organization to change, it needs to have the willingness to adapt. With willingness comes admitting there is a problem around stress. Employees need to understand the problem—not just address it by saying they need a gym membership. They need to figure out why their organization's culture produces stress and get recommendations on how to make a change.

For your organization to adapt, you need a plan to take incremental steps toward shifting the culture to support wellness and well-being. Some of your culture changes will come about as you apply techniques in the next three chapters of this book, particularly getting leadership buy-in and employee engagement. Culture change is not a quick fix but a long haul that builds over time and involves everyone in your organization.

DEFINING A HAPPY, HEALTHY CULTURE

A happy, healthy culture is one where an organization's way of working nurtures and supports the well-being of its employees. A Happy, Healthy Nonprofit values self-care and builds WE-care programs, activities, and cues around group activities to address well-being. A happy, healthy culture leads to high morale and peak productivity and attracts and retains top talent resulting in a high-performing organization. You have to think of organizational culture as the creation of conditions for a habitat of vitality that allows happy and healthy to thrive.

As Carter McNamara, MBA, PhD, of Authenticity Consulting says: "A nonprofit's culture is its personality."[4] You experience the culture of your nonprofit when you enter your workplace and view the layout, see what people are wearing and how they behave, and feel whether the energy is calm or chaotic. Your nonprofit's personality can be happy and healthy or miserable and exhausted.

Behavior that reflects your organization's culture happens even without anyone consulting the employee handbook. Employees inherently know when they should leave the office early because they are stressed out or when they'd be better off unplugging from e-mails over the weekend. But they neglect these self-care activities and mirror the actions of others in the organization, staying late because everyone else is still working, or checking e-mails over the weekend because their boss is e-mailing them.

Even when there are specific statements in the employee handbook addressing overtime, working from home, vacation time, and other ways of work, those statements are meaningless if no one pays attention to that document. When policies and behaviors are in direct conflict with one another, stress and dysfunction win over self-care and productivity.

The Emotional Side of Happy, Healthy Culture

A 16-month longitudinal research study titled "What's Love Got to Do with It? A Longitudinal Study of the Culture of Companionate Love and Employee and Client Outcomes in the Long-Term Care Setting" set out to measure the influence of emotional well-being and behavior of both employees and patients at a long-term health care facility. The study, conducted by Wharton management professor Sigal Barsade and assistant professor of management at George Mason University Olivia "Mandy" O'Neill, looked at 185 employees, 108 patients, and 42 of those patients' family members. The researchers' big question was:

> Can an organizational culture of happiness, compassion, and love lead to better results?

They found that an emotional culture of "companionate love" or genuine bonds among coworkers—where employees demonstrate caring, compassion, tenderness, and affection for one another—was associated with lower burnout and stress levels. A compassionate culture was not only more engaging but was essential to employee morale, teamwork, and patient satisfaction. In other words, if employees were happy and worked together more compassionately, the organization was more successful. Creating a culture where everyone treats one another with compassion lowers everyone's stress levels.[5]

According to Barbara Fredrickson, a professor of psychology at the University of North Carolina at Chapel Hill, strong connections with others create a sense of safety and capacity that become fuel for professional development and growth. These high-quality connections are what Fredrickson calls "micro-moments of connection." When these connections take place, staff thinking broadens, they absorb knowledge more quickly, their skills are enhanced, or they are inspired to make changes. Connected employees are more engaged, playful, open, and resilient in the face of stress. These micro-moments can accumulate to make a positive impact on people's overall health and quality of life.

The Case for Employee Engagement

Jennifer Flynn, health management strategy consultant at the Mayo Clinic, said in an interview in Laura Putnam's book, *Workplace Wellness that Works,* that key to employees engaging in their own health is "perceived organizational support." That is, "if employees do not feel supported by their organization, by their manager, or by their coworkers, they are less likely to trust and therefore engage with any wellness efforts on a meaningful level."

A report called "The State of the American Workplace: Employee Engagement Insights for U.S. Business Leaders"[6] categorizes engaged employees on the following continuum:

1. *Engaged employees* are passionate, feeling profound connections to their company, driving it forward.
2. *Not engaged employees* are "checked out sleepwalking through their workday, not putting energy or passion into their work.
3. *Actively disengaged employees* are unhappy at work, acting out their unhappiness, undermining their engaged coworkers' accomplishments.

You have probably heard the saying "Culture eats strategy for breakfast" attributed to famed management guru Peter Drucker. Culture is the underpinning of everything your organization is trying to accomplish. Culture is the driving force behind your organization's vision, mission, and values. Culture can make or break your organization from the inside out. Without addressing your organization's culture, your staff will eat french fries for breakfast and not the healthy snacks in the break room!

Elements of Culture Change

Organizational culture change involves a shift in your nonprofit's personality and emotional culture but needs an assessment process, education, and changes to structures and processes to make it stick. In Chapter 3, we introduced you to ways of changing your personal habits to happier, healthier ones. Remember how hard it was to change a personal habit like going from skimping on sleep to prioritizing seven to nine hours each night? When you try to create an organizational cultural shift, keep in mind you are not just trying to get one person to change but everyone in your organization.

"Changing culture isn't as simple as identifying the new behaviors you want to see and articulating a new set of beliefs and values associated with these," notes Bridgespan's Kirk Kramer in the article "Strategies for Changing Your Organization's Culture."[7] Nobody said it would be easy!

In *Workplace Wellness that Works*, Putnam uses the following framework to better understand organizational culture and the potential to shift it into a culture of well-being. The framework is based on Abraham Maslow's hierarchy of needs, mapped to an organization's hierarchy of needs:

- Level 1: Functioning Factor—Do people have what they need to do their job?
- Level 2: Feelings Factor—Do people feel appreciated and respected?
- Level 3: Friendship Factor—Do people feel connected to one another?
- Level 4: Forward Factor—Do people feel like they have opportunities for growth?
- Level 5: Fulfillment Factor—Do people feel like they are inspired and working toward a higher purpose?[8]

Nonprofit organizations often naturally provide the Fulfillment Factor due to the mission-driven nature of the work. Brian Scios, director of community and communications for Childhood Domestic Violence Association, talks about how people who work for nonprofits are there to do good in the world. They want and get meaning in their lives by going to work every day, working for the greater good. "But then they discover limited budgets, staffing, and mission creep to follow the money," says Scios. "The advice I give to any new employees who get frustrated: Do something about it. Bring up your concerns, try to come up with solutions, and work to get them implemented."

Scios's advice should be a rallying cry for all nonprofit professionals but also for the organizations that employ them. Your organization should listen to your employees, their complaints, and their needs, and not just pay lip service to what they tell you but actually address their concerns. Your employees have a front row seat to the culture dysfunction in your organization, and their feedback should not be ignored. Acting on employee feedback fosters employee engagement and, even better, initiates important organizational culture changes.

When you look at Level 2 on the hierarchy, the Feelings Factor, examine what it feels like to work at your nonprofit. Do people feel appreciated or are they afraid? Do they feel energized or depleted? Justin Chase, president of Crisis Response Network, a suicide prevention line, knew he was not going to be able to implement a WE-care strategy unless the organization's culture changed. When he was hired as the second executive director, he saw that the workplace culture was fear-based, regulatory, and top down.

"The employee voice was frowned upon. And anytime senior management was seen in the workplace, it was to fire people," says Chase. "My process was to be very transparent and get feedback from employees. I heard a lot about how people were scared to come to work and fearful about change." Working with an employee engagement committee, Chase systematically made changes within the organization based on employee feedback. We discuss his techniques in Chapter 9.

Sandra Bass, PhD, assistant dean of students and director at the University of California Berkeley Public Service Center, says the center works at creating a culture where the students feel connected to one another, addressing Level 3, the Friendship Factor.

Says Bass, "We use play to encourage joy, laughter, and lightness—it is a communal way of addressing some of the stress that comes with social justice work. For example, have a space with comfortable chairs, adult coloring books, and nice music. It is a place for students to destress and connect with one another if they are stressed. It creates a space for students to create a community of care."

Pamela Chaloult, chief opportunity officer at BALLE, an organization that researches well-being in the workplace, says her own organization has created a culture that fosters staff well-being. Doing so makes sense because their organizational core values are based around transformational experiences in the workplace. When new staff members join their team, they already understand that employees respect one another. Everyone treats each other with loving kindness.

Says Chaloult, "We have a hugging culture. We greet each other with hugs. Physical hugging increases endorphins, and it is a way for connection."

Chaloult admits that hugging may seem unusual in the workplace, but it works for them. Staff is also encouraged to give respectful feedback to one another coming from "a place of appreciation."

Nonprofits often face challenges with providing Level 4, the Forward Factor or opportunities to move forward, whether this is the chance for career advancement or opportunities for professional development. Lynnae Brown, director of the Howie the Harp Advocacy Center, a social service agency that provides mental health services in New York, says, "We view staff jobs like a well paid internship—where staff are learning, building capacity, and strengthening skills as they contribute so they can move on to greater pastures. Our program staff is small—10 to 12—so there isn't a lot of room to move up or even around. We all did the StrengthFinder assessment to understand our personal strengths and this led to an appreciation of what we all contributed to the program. From there, each staff person created their own professional development and growth plan based on 'big picture' goals."

Initiating Happy, Healthy Culture Change

Understanding culture change is one thing. Getting the culture shift going is another. It takes time, process, and patience as staff and founders from GlobalGiving can attest. Several years ago, GlobalGiving facilitated an all-staff workshop where they named and made explicit their core values. Their values included: Always Open; Never Settle; Committed to Wow; and Listen, Act, Learn, Repeat. It was not long before the organization's values—like Never Settle—made staff feel stretched and conflicted about their work-life balance. Staff hit a bit of a crisis point, according to Alison Carlman, director of marketing and communications.

Carlman recalls, "Our executive team heard what the staff was saying, and they allocated time and funding for us to design our own process for identifying our challenges and recommending solutions."

Staff set out to answer questions like:

- How can we create a safety net to support us when we feel overwhelmed by our values?
- How should we navigate the absolutes like *never* and *always* that are part of our values?
- How do we balance what makes sense for our mission and vision and what makes cents for our nonprofit business?

Their staff spent a day with a facilitator and came up with some strategies to change their way of working that balanced excellence without excessive work hours and stress. The organization also instituted time and project management systems and tools to help staff avoid stressful work flows and commitments. But more important, says Carlman, "The executive team invested resources into guest speakers, short courses, tools, and staff over the course of a year to help us all become more confident at listening, experimenting, learning, and pivoting or persevering. It has created a workplace that is fun, dynamic, and sustainable."

Creating a happy, healthy nonprofit culture requires a step-by-step approach. Here are some key steps:

Step 1. Awareness: Inform everyone within your organization about the issue of stress and burnout and the importance of self-care. Share the science from credible sources to back up the information you provide. For individuals, frame the conversation of self-care as more than addressing physical health but providing energy and vitality in all aspects of life. For organizations, frame the conversation around the benefits of investing in a happy, healthy culture that includes reduced health costs and major boosts in productivity, employee engagement, and talent attraction and retention.

Step 2. Learning: Create the space and time for assessment and education for employees and help them develop their own customized self-care plans based on the results of their individual assessments. Bring in experts to provide workshops, lunch and learn sessions, brainstorming sessions, interactive retreats, and webinars on self-care topics. Offer short-term sessions that teach stress management techniques like meditation, deep breathing, or yoga that can have long-term effects. Make sure leadership takes part in these activities to encourage wider participation.

Step 3. Practice: For employees to alter their self-care habits, they need to feel empowered and supported. Remember that education and activities only go so far without employee engagement or an organizational culture that supports individual efforts. Frame this culture change as your organization's challenge, not as a problem for specific staff members to tackle. Foster the "we are all in this together" feeling to set the stage that allows people to talk about these changes and to support one another. We can't say this enough: Leadership must model some of the new behaviors. When leaders take care of themselves, others follow and your organization benefits.

Step 4. Accountability: Turn to your assessment results and retake the assessments after a period of time to see what progress has been made. Set up regular activities for self-care as part of the office work routine such as check-ins about well-being during staff meetings, opportunities to debrief after particularly stressful organizational deadlines or situations, and mentorship between staff members. Encourage staff to find "accountability buddies" to support each other's quest to be happier and healthier.

Don't think of the goal of WE-care as starting a traditional wellness program. WE-care is bigger than that. You are embarking on creating and implementing more than an incentive activity or a new health care benefit. You are changing entrenched attitudes, behaviors, and bad habits that are perpetuated across your entire organization and bringing down morale, energy, and productivity. WE-care is a collaborative process to develop and sustain a culture of internal well-being.

THE ROLE OF THE LEADERS

In 2013, the Meyer Foundation[9] conducted a year-long research effort interviewing 100 executive directors of grantee organizations to better understand how to support their leadership. The research revealed that 50 percent of organizational leaders saw a link between their professional development and personal well-being and the effectiveness of their organizations. Seventy-nine percent of executive directors were engaging in activities that improved their personal well-being; 65 percent engaged in activities that improved their physical well-being; and 49 percent engaged in spiritual activities. More nonprofit leaders understand that they need to take care of themselves because self-care is the vital link between enhancing both their leadership abilities and their organization's impact.

Business guru Peter F. Drucker asserted that the responsibility for setting the tone of an organization—the culture—rests with the leader: someone who has high expectations for performance and results, acts with integrity and expects others to do the same, and shows genuine concern for all employees. According to Drucker, these leadership qualities create an effective organization because others will emulate the leader's behavior.[10]

NetSuite Director of Social Impact Peggy Duvette, who worked as an executive director at a nonprofit for many years, says, "If an executive director does not take care of himself or herself, it is very likely that the staff will do the same. It is so important that as nonprofit leaders, we drive the path for social impact but also healthy careers."

As an organizational leader, Mari Kuraishi, cofounder and president of GlobalGiving, is committed to seeing her organization achieve impact through the way everyone does his or her work. "I can't expect staff to listen to me if I don't walk the talk. I used to be a serious workaholic. There were long stretches of time when I didn't get home until 9:00 or 10:00 every evening and spent weekends at the office. But I have consciously dialed that back as I have gotten older, leaving the office at 5:00 P.M., getting exercise in the middle of the day, and, most recently, taking a sabbatical. Ultimately, if we have healthier and—it's hoped—happier employees, they will be in a position to make our clients' lives better."

In the book, *Contagious Culture,* author Anese Cavanaugh describes how leader mind-sets, attitudes, behaviors, and energy—positive and negative—can rub off on their staff. She explains "contagious" as how a leader makes staff feel and how they behave based on the leader's presence. If a leader is happy, the staff feels it. If a leader is stressed out, the staff feels it. Staff members not only feel what a leader is feeling, but internalize the attitude and pay it forward in their behavior, whether good or bad.[11]

Kuraishi knows that when she models work-life balance, it rubs off on GlobalGiving's staff. Says GlobalGiving's Alison Carlman, "We often hear the phrase, 'be the change you wish to see in the world,' and self-care is at the heart of that. Change on a big scale can't happen without change at the staff level, including the CEO. It's just as much about developing ourselves as it is about developing the people, communities, and cities we intend to help. If we're not growing in tandem and in relationship, then it will always be an unequal, unhealthy partnership."

Since 2006, The Duke Endowment has supported a growing movement to promote a culture of wellness inside of hospitals, with an emphasis on programs and cultural cues that ensure healthy choices are easier to make. The hospital workplaces were assessed on different indicators, including employee participation in the programs, and there was a resulting report card with grades.

"The big insight we learned is that when the CEOs signed on, staff used the programs, made healthier choices, and their overall health grades improved—but only when leadership was engaged," explains Meka S. Sales, program officer for health care grants at The Duke Endowment, who also helps manage the foundation's internal wellness program.

One nonprofit staffer from an educational foundation shared a story about how culture can be contagious in a way that is destructive to self-care. In her job orientation, she was informed that the organization is run like a start-up, so she was to expect to work long, hard hours. The executive director, she was told, would e-mail staff between midnight and 3:00 A.M.

"And if you didn't respond, he would let you know that he was very hard working, and you were not," recalls the staffer. To deal with stress, she meditated and practiced yoga regularly. "But I was constantly questioned about why I didn't seem stressed enough. I was told that I wasn't working hard enough because I wasn't stressed out."

At one point, this staffer suggested to the executive director that all staff consider some practices like yoga or meditation to reduce stress.

"He rejected the idea because it would get in the way of getting work done," she recalls. "It was awful to see that taking care of your stress equated to goofing off. Eventually, I had to leave this job because of the culture."

Amber Hacker, vice president of operations and communications, and Julia Smith, marketing and communications manager at Interfaith Youth Core, recount a story about the importance of leadership making self-care a cultural norm. They received feedback from staff about the types of activities that might help them avoid burnout. Many of their staff members told them that, sometimes, they just needed some "creativity time" to do things away from the office. The organization formalized creativity time, putting it in their employee handbook and establishing a policy that staff members take three creativity time hours per month.

The organization made great efforts to listen to employees and support them. Hacker said no one was actually using this creativity time, because no one on the senior management team was participating. As a result, staff didn't feel as if they had permission to use it.

"After an executive team member sent out an e-mail to everyone to remind them about this benefit and also shared that he was planning to visit an art museum as part of their creativity time, staff members started to use this benefit," says Hacker.

Self-care is just as important for leaders as it is for all staff, and leaders can initiate concrete changes within their organizations to help shift the culture and promote self-care.

"For me, I feel like I have to demonstrate self-care, self-awareness, develop and/or clarify boundaries and expectations, and foster certain language that supports all that," explains Lynnae Brown. Brown says her organization isn't developing a wellness program per se but is "incorporating awareness of self-care and wellness as part of being an effective employee."

For example, in the center's employee handbook, there is talk about how developing hobbies, having outside interests, taking vacations, and the like can enhance work-life balance. The handbook also states that expecting work to fulfill personal emotional needs isn't a good idea.

"We encourage each other to take vacations, plan 'mental health' days, go to doctor appointments, work efficiently within an eight-hour workday, and take our lunch breaks," says Brown. "I think those distinctions are necessary because of the unspoken but very strong vibe in social services that you are to sweat, slave, and run yourself into the ground for no money. I don't think that's healthy or just."

Brown adds that she doesn't want her organization to be responsible for staff's actual wellness, either. They teach their students about self-directed wellness so, she says, their staff needs to model it as well.

Nonprofit consultant and blogger Joan Garry, who spent many years as a nonprofit CEO, says, "You know that kids' game Follow the Leader? The self-care ball is in our court: go home at a reasonable hour, call a staff break at 3:00 P.M., and actually waste some time talking about what everyone is binge watching. And please, stop sending e-mails at 5:00 A.M.!"

As we've heard from Kuraishi, Brown, Garry, and other nonprofit leaders, modeling self-care and paying attention to their own work-life balance is important for the good of their entire organizations.

Happy, Healthy Leadership in Practice

What does leadership modeling at an organization look like in practical terms? How can leaders lead the charge so all staff models happy, healthy behaviors at the office and to the people and communities they serve? They can do so by practicing healthy leadership and talking with staff about self-care, not just modeling it.

Kara Allen Soldati, president and CEO of United Friends, admits that she did not share enough about how she personally approached the concept of work-life balance and self-care at her previous job. While she did integrate flex work policies, adjusted schedules to meet staff needs, implemented paid volunteer time, and raised time off allowances, a review by some of her staff and board members revealed to her that she didn't effectively explain how she prioritized her own self-care or communicate how she wanted others in the organization to do so as well.

When she arrived at her new position, Allen Soldati embarked on a "listening tour" to hear from others throughout the organization. She made a point to share a personal example of her self-care strategies with each person, and she asked them two questions:

1. How do you model self-care?
2. What could our wellness plan include that would ensure that you and our teammates are most fulfilled and modeling this to our young people as well?

Allen Soldati found it was effective to not only model self-care, but to start the conversation around self-care at her organization. Torrie Dunlap, CEO of Kids Included Together, made a deliberate plan to spread self-care throughout her organization. Dunlap noticed that her organization's very passionate staff was falling in the all-too-familiar trap of putting their work before their own health and wellness.

She researched corporate wellness practices and interviewed wellness consultants to develop a program to encourage everyone at her organization to lead healthier lives. On a nonprofit budget, they could not afford extravagant measures such as catered organic lunches and weekly massages. Dunlap instead identified a list of healthy—and affordable—activities that everyone, including herself, could take part in. She also considered how to give permission to staff to be healthy at work.

Says Dunlap, "A light bulb went off. What if we made physical activity a part of people's paid time at work?" She worked with her senior leadership team to put together a plan for her entire staff, including senior leaders. It included:

- Three paid hours off per week to exercise, and the employee must match that with two hours per week on their own time.
- Adding exercise time to their work calendar so people could monitor how they were progressing.

Her organization offered these things as a three-month pilot and made them optional to anyone who wanted to take part. They also asked staff to log their exercise hours and track outcomes. At the end of three months, they took a survey of all participants. All of them reported feeling a reduction in stress. They also tested biometrics like blood pressure, cholesterol, and other indicators and saw positive outcomes. One staff member was able to successfully discontinue her diabetes medication under her doctor's supervision.

The important thing, notes Dunlap, is staff reported they felt the organization truly cared about their health, and it wasn't just talk. Dunlap adds the program has been a successful recruiting tool for new talent. "Candidates for new positions have told us that the charge to exercise during the workday is an attractive perk."

Improving internal and external relationships, enhancing employee wellness and well-being, and attracting and retaining talent are just a few of the benefits of WE-care in the workplace. People-focused leaders know this and make self-care part of strategy. But they can't operate in a vacuum. They still have to answer to their boards.

Board Buy-In

To make a happy, healthy organizational culture sustainable, it has to be endorsed, nurtured, and supported at the top. A nonprofit's board of directors has a fiduciary responsibility for the nonprofit and its mission. To succeed with culture change over the long term, the board members must become stewards for ensuring that their staff is taking care of themselves. Yet too many times the board's leadership compounds the stress levels in the organization.

Says one nonprofit executive director, "In our organization, we try to maintain work balance, but every quarter before a board meeting, the entire staff is paralyzed preparing for the meeting. You can feel the fear."

Dr. Suzanne Allen, president and CEO of Philanthropy Ohio, addressed the topic of self-care with her board by integrating it into the strategic planning process for her organization. By doing so, she involved her board in the discussions from the start. She asked her board to consider this tactic: ensure all staff has the energy and appropriate professional development for sustainable performance as part of a retention strategy.

"It was a tough sell. They felt that 'ensuring energy' was a bit vague because people come to work to work," admits Allen. "As a relatively new leader of an organization, I've learned that this is the only thing I really can do for my staff. To create a culture that rewards ulcers is not only *not* creative, it is not sustainable. My leadership team and I shared with our staff—and with the board—that this is important to us, and [staff] professional and personal development plans should reflect the desire we all have for their continued growth and renewal."

Scaling a happy, healthy culture begins in the boardroom. Changing the culture starts with a board conversation. Board members need to understand and endorse the importance of self-care as part of the organization's strategic goals and way of working. Says Hildy Gottlieb of Creating the Future, "We have spent many board meetings hammering out policies and processes for ensuring that we are bringing out the best in our staff." In Chapter 9, we'll discuss well-being policies in more details.

SUPPORTING EMPLOYEES FOR CULTURE CHANGE

Introducing self-care into your nonprofit includes encouraging staff to self-assess and create their own self-care plans. The materials we've included in Chapter 3 can be easily incorporated into your organization's internal communications and employee handbook. Education, coaching, and peer-to-peer-support are important parts of your happy, healthy strategy and can also be beneficial for culture change.

Education and Coaching

Put simply, if you want people to change, they have to understand the reason for it and why it is important. That's why informational seminars and one-on-one health coaching are the backbone of culture change as well as being a component of workplace wellness and well-being programs. These educational activities are part of a strategy to shift the organization's culture to embrace happy, healthy ways of working.

"Walking as work" is part of the organization culture at The United Way in Sioux Falls, South Dakota. Every day at 10:00 A.M. and 2:00 P.M., everyone at work leaves the office and walks a mile together. That's every day of the year. The walk takes 15 minutes. In warm weather, they walk in a nearby park. In cold weather, they walk the hallways in their building complex. This daily practice has been in place at the organization for 15 years.

How did it come about? The agency initially brought in a health coach to counsel employees on a quarterly basis as part of its wellness program. Some of the discussions focused on the importance of avoiding the dangers of a sedentary work style. The walking breaks began as an experiment and became an integral part of the way they work.

The Humane Society of the United States (HSUS) offers employee education and training as part of its wellness program. Every year, the organization identifies a wellness theme—topics like vegan nutrition or financial wellness—and hosts a series of free webinars related to the theme. If employees participate, they receive points that give them a discount on their health insurance plans. According to Cecilia Royal, senior manager of the organization's HR department, HSUS also provides wellness coaching to employees who request it.

Offering workshops and webinars is not enough. Pairing these with individual coaching for those who need the extra guidance helps change take hold. Bringing vendors in from the outside to provide this support may not always be financially viable. Luckily, there are other ways to shore up staff efforts to make positive strides toward happy and healthy.

Group and Peer-to-Peer Learning Support

Building and sustaining new habits among your diverse staff requires a multilayered approach that keeps everyone motivated. Peer support or positive peer pressure is a potent force when it comes to shaping happy and healthy in the workplace, plus it is cost-effective if expense is a concern. Bryce Williams, vice president of well-being at Blue Shield of California, says of wellness support that "peer-to-peer equals results."[12] When you work at an organization where positive behavior is viewed as the norm, where it is encouraged, rewarded, and expected, it influences your behavior and seeps into your daily routine.

Gretchen Rubin, author of *Better Than Before*, says that one of the best ways to build good habits is to join or start a group for people who have the common goal of changing their habits. She notes that habit groups have many benefits, including exchanging ideas, providing energy, and giving encouragement. More important, a habit group offers the secret sauce to habit change: accountability. One way to start a peer-to-peer model is through "accountability partners," where two peers in your organization meet regularly to celebrate achievements and work through challenges.

Rubin says while accountability partners can work, she doesn't think pairs offer the same stability as groups. If there are only two people and one person loses interest, gets distracted, or is absent for a time, the accountability benefit disappears. With a group, you're not as dependent on one person's engagement.[13]

A peer support group is a group of employees who can learn from each other and provide a structured environment where people who share self-care goals can safely discuss their experiences and learn from one another. Research shows that talking with others who have been through similar experiences may make all the difference in sticking with something like habit change.[14] Lucy Nolan, executive director of End Hunger CT!, says her staff supports each other as an informal accountability group for healthy diet and exercise. "One staff member quit drinking 10 sodas a day and started to exercise and has lost a lot of weight," says Nolan.

According to Blue Shield of California, employees are more likely to participate in a wellness program if a work colleague invites them. Their commitment to their self-care plan is deepened if there is peer-to-peer accountability. Having a peer group component as part of your wellness strategy can:

- Increase motivation
- Reduce stress and anxiety

- Boost confidence in sustaining new habits
- Remove barriers to forming new habits

Incorporating peer engagement models in a strategy for embracing wellness and well-being increases the chance of success.

"Peer support can build in accountability and commonality, reduce isolation, and provide encouragement and connection while providing guidance from the more experienced for the less experienced. We have different types of groups for patients with different diagnoses such as diabetes or post–heart attack. They offer an instant social network and access to other perspectives," says Tina Kenyon, LICSW, ACSW, and faculty at New Hampshire Dartmouth Family Medicine Residency at Concord Hospital, who has over 23 years of experience facilitating peer groups for health professionals including teaching stress reduction practices and work-life balance strategies.

Kenyon adds, "As far as influencing organizational culture, one factor is whether or not a group coming together with common goals and aspirations directly impacts their ability to establish and reinforce a positive culture."

Kenyon has observed dramatic results in the peer groups of medical students she facilitates:

> They learn they are not alone in their struggle, and that bringing one's humanity into daily work can be so powerful. Through supporting one another, they tap into their own resilience, and connect with the resilience in peers and patients. We hear from graduates, now in residency after medical school, that they realize what a key role peer support played in preventing burnout and maintaining a sense of hope in many situations.

Peer-to-peer and group support provide the cultural cues and prompts for employees to regularly practice self-care at work, contributing to a happy, healthy culture. Based on the results of your organizational assessments and what your staff determines should be in their self-care plans, map educational topics to employee needs. Then determine if one-on-one coaching is viable. Even if it isn't, you can still form pairs and groups to provide additional support for habit change and fundamental culture change.

COMMITTING TO CULTURE CHANGE

To ensure the activities you design for your wellness and well-being plans are accepted, adopted, supported, and celebrated, you need to shift your organization's culture. While informational sessions, coaching, and peer and group support can help educate and motivate staff to adopt happy, healthy habits, only culture change will make it last. Take a few moments to reflect on your organization's current culture with these questions:

- What is our organization's culture?
- What people or actions have helped define our culture?
- How do our board, executive director, and senior leaders affect our organization's culture?
- How engaged is our staff?
- What are some of the main causes of stress within our organization?
- What policies or ways that we work do we need to change to reduce stress?
- What activities does our organization need to implement to reduce stress?
- What is our organizational attitude toward self-care, health, well-being, and happiness at work?
- How do we respond to individuals within our organization who engage in self-care?
- Who are the internal organization champions of the idea of a happy, healthy program?
- What are some immediate changes we could propose to put into place at work to gauge need?
- How will we get leadership buy-in, and what can their roles be in supporting the wellness initiatives?
- Who will address the concept of wellness programs with our organization's board?
- What can we do if we are unable to get board support?

Culture change comes from myriad efforts including modeling, incorporating rituals, using communications and incentives, collaborating with staff, making changes to work flow, and even developing policies and programs. Once you change your organization's culture for the better, you can develop a Happy, Healthy Strategy that fits your new and improved culture. The next two chapters include examples of the elements you can put in place to make WE-care your organization's norm.

CHAPTER 7

The Activities and Cues

Self-Care to WE-Care

How's that donor retention report coming?

WE-CARE IN THE WORKPLACE

We remember seeing a viral tweet from entrepreneur Randi Zuckerberg that touches on why organizations need WE-care. "The entrepreneur's dilemma: Maintaining friendships. Building a great company. Spending time with family. Staying fit. Getting sleep. Pick three." This dilemma is all too common for nonprofit professionals as well. In this chapter, we focus on activities and cues that you can integrate into your workplace well-being initiatives to help address this dilemma. Activities are events that require participation designed to support organizational well-being for greater productivity and morale boosts. Cues are environmental reminders that make happy and healthy choices easier for employees to make.

Workplace activities are typically group undertakings in the form of programs that help your staff work together to acquire self-care habits and practices. Activities can be introduced into every aspect of your organization—from the C-suite to teams across all departments as well as at all-staff meetings and events. They can take place on-site at your organization's workplace or off-site—for example, offering a gym discount at the local YMCA—but well-being activities are definitely not just about the discounts.

When identifying and designing activities for your organization, keep in mind the following guidelines:

- Identify the value proposition for employees.
- Understand individual employee motivations and barriers to participation, and design programs accordingly.
- Align activities with productivity outcomes.
- Link to measurable results and measure.

Cues can be visuals like signs in physical areas including hallways, walls, elevators, stairwells, offices, and common spaces or take digital form such as screen savers, e-mails, and documents or videos on an intranet. Cues can be words or images but can also be sounds and even music. For example, when it is time for everyone at The United Way in Sioux Falls, South Dakota, to pause work and walk a mile together, a bell rings. Do Something in New York City holds "Toto Tuesdays" where they encourage staff to leave the office on time by playing Toto's 1980s hit "Africa" until everyone goes home.

Activities and cues don't have to break your nonprofit's budget. Check with your health insurance company representative to see if it offers resources, incentives, and packaged programs to help you easily plan and implement well-being activities and cues for your WE-care as part of your health care benefits package. Community organizations like your local YMCA, chapter of the American Heart Association, hospital, and other groups may offer free or low-cost programs, activities, and materials you can use.

If your organization tries to launch random activities without support from senior leadership or feedback and participation from employees, participation will likely be disappointingly low. One associate director of a mental health agency told us how excited she was when one of her new employees instituted a Tuesday afternoon yoga and meditation class. When we checked back with her several months later to see how it was going, she told us, "We have not been doing yoga nor meditation at work. There wasn't much buy-in from employees, and the busy-ness of the day has taken over our Tuesday afternoons."

On reflection, she told us, "There was not enough motivation to sustain participation. We needed to have senior leadership and the organization make yoga or mindfulness a priority so that it was okay to participate and not just give it lip service."

We've heard many similar stories about nonprofits rushing to implement a well-being activity or program but neglecting to get leadership on board or to consult with staff. According to Melanie Duppins, VP of human capital and teacher outreach at DonorsChoose, the most successful initiatives for her organization happen when the executive team holds conversations about what staff wants. Then leadership empowers staff to take the lead.

Well-intentioned but piecemeal programming won't gain the same kind of traction as a well-organized series of programs based on a larger Happy, Healthy Strategy. See Chapter 9 for tips on developing your overarching strategy. Addressing the Wellness Triad of sleep, nutrition, and exercise is a great place to start to stretch and strengthen your organization's happy and healthy muscles, even at the office.

Sleep Activities and Cues

Sleep in the workplace may seem like an oxymoron, and sleeping on the job can be a bad thing. But without enough sleep, employees are unable to focus or perform simple tasks and lack patience. People who are cranky from lack of sleep are not fun to be around. Studies show that daytime napping can elevate moods and even improve immune function.[1] Napping during the day can improve cognitive functioning, leading to greater productivity at work.[2] When concentration wanes in the late afternoon and early evening, experts suggest taking a 20-minute nap to prevent an energy dip.

In other parts of the world, midday naps are an important part of the culture and are viewed as crucial to the productivity of employees. Lester F. Coutinho, deputy director at the Gates Foundations, noted, "I grew up in Goa, India, where all the businesses and markets closed from 2:00 P.M. to 4:00 P.M. for siesta. This is still practiced as a way of being *susegado* or easy going in a nonderogatory way."

In the for-profit sector, a growing number of corporations such as Google, Apple, Zappos, AOL, Time Warner, Facebook, GlaxoSmithKline, Procter & Gamble, and Nike offer employees napping rooms or "sleep pods," small enclosed spaces that make office napping private and convenient.[3] Some have even invested in "nap desks"[4] or "napping chairs."[5] Arianna Huffington, author of *Sleep Revolution*, is a champion of getting enough sleep and even put employee nap rooms in the offices of the *Huffington Post*.

In contrast, in the nonprofit sector, nap rooms or sleep pods are extremely rare. Some nonprofit professionals we interviewed use power naps to restore their energy, even if it is not an activity sanctioned by their organizations. Says one nonprofit professional, "I used to nap on the floor under a desk at my nonprofit, but I always felt like I was sneaking."

Evonne Heyning, a tech and media strategy consultant producing with ExO (Exponential Organizations), recalls, "At my first nonprofit job, I would take a walk during my lunch break or just lie on a blanket out on the lawn of our office compound. It wasn't an official policy." Says Jen Bokoff, director of knowledge services at Foundation Center, "There's a couch in my office, and I regularly close my eyes on it. But napping is not a formal part of our organizational policy."

Meka S. Sales, health care program officer at The Duke Endowment, serves on an employee committee that oversees the endowment's well-being in the workplace initiatives. As part of the voluntary program, employees wear trackers that monitor not only fitness activity but also sleep. The organization holds monthly challenges including a sleep challenge. Participants said they gained a lot of awareness of their sleep habits and could improve them. Says Sales, "Trackers have become a cultural norm, and there is a lot of water cooler conversation around people exchanging how much sleep they get."

Sleep is critical to doing good work. Having conversations about sleep at work, accommodating rest time and even midday naps, and building sleep challenges into other health-related challenges are just some of the ways of elevating the value of sleep at your organization. Your organization will reap the rewards of a well-rested staff!

Nutrition Activities and Cues

Good nutrition is also critical for working effectively and starts with knowing what to eat and what to avoid. At home, you may be successful at avoiding sugary snacks because you didn't put them into your shopping cart at the store so they are not readily available in your kitchen. But at work, if there are chocolate covered doughnuts in the conference room at a staff meeting, you might be more tempted to indulge, especially if the CEO is stuffing his or her face with the sugary treat.

Cindy Leonard, a trainer at the Bayer Center, says, "Our nonprofit conducts a lot of events and workshops. The leftovers, naturally, are put in the fridge for staff to consume. Some leftovers, like carrots and humus, are healthy, but the potato chips and cookies are not snacks I want to eat. It challenges my discipline of trying to eat in a healthy way."

Having a plan for making healthy foods and beverages available at the office is an effective well-being activity, and placing them prominently in the break room can act as a cue to help everyone make better nutritional choices.

Carole Caplan, formerly with Fair Food Network, a nonprofit that focuses on a more sustainable and just food system, says their staff lived, or rather ate, the organization's mission every day.

"The lack of a microwave and daily use of the stove brought the aroma of what our work was all about directly into the workplace. We exchanged ideas and recipes, and we celebrated successes with homemade pickles and locally brewed beer."

Providing healthy foods at meetings doesn't take any more effort than providing unhealthy food. Amy Sample Ward, executive director of NTEN, says their office is near a weekly farmer's market so it's convenient to pick up a bag of fresh fruit for weekly staff meetings. Also, Ward is vigilant about serving gluten-free options including at NTEN-sponsored events and board meetings.

The Kaiser Permanente Healthy Meetings Guide offers 15 tips for light meals and snacks that are simple and low cost. They recommend putting the food on a side table so it's harder to reach for second helpings. The American Heart Association's (AHA) Healthy Workplace Food and Beverage Toolkit provides nutritional guidance for food in the workplace and practical action tips that are also low cost to implement.

With long work hours, grabbing food from vending machines is all too common at nonprofits. Because vending machines are visible and convenient, the AHA recommends in its tool kit to improve the nutritional quality of vending machine selections. Provide healthy vending machine snacks as a sign that your organization cares about the health of your employees. The individual and organizational benefits are worth it!

Here's an activity: Why not celebrate "National Eating Healthy Day," the first Wednesday in November, to raise awareness at your organization about the importance of good nutrition and good eating decisions? The American Heart Association sponsors the event and also provides a free tool kit specifically about this event. Even if participation is optional in these types of organization-wide activities, some benefits will inevitably rub off on nonparticipants through the power of positive influence.

For a more regular activity, consider combining healthy eating with communal meals like Pathways to Education Canada, an organization that helps low-income youth transition to college.

"As an experiment, we decided to pick up a crockpot from the Canadian Craigslist, and that was the beginning of Crockpot Mondays," explains Jason Shim, associate director, digital strategy and alumni relations at Pathways. "All meals must be vegan and gluten-free, and the food must be consumed with others in the staff kitchen—no grabbing and going. Crockpot Mondays is part of the fabric of Pathways because people mention it to job candidates as a perk of working at our organization. Crockpot Mondays has allowed our 50-member staff to share their culinary talents, as well as connect with one another over meals that have been meticulously prepared." NTEN's Ward says, "I noticed that staff often eat at their desks because we do a lot of webinars or remote meetings. So we decided to have a weekly communal healthy brown bag lunch on Thursdays. We have remote staff, so we bring them in via a Google Hangout, and they join us at the table."

Eating together, and the social interaction of shared meals, provides many boosts to individual well-being. Collaborating on meals and breaking bread also builds and strengthens relationships, a boon to any organization. When those meals are healthy, everyone wins.

Exercise Activities and Cues

Exercise programs are probably one of the most common initiatives or employee benefits implemented to promote workplace well-being. Fitness activities can take a number of forms depending on everything from your office location to your organization's budget to staff size to employee interest. We encourage you to get creative and not just do fitness as usual. Christine Egger, a nonprofit consultant, says, "I think the trick is to integrate fitness and exercise into your workday." We agree!

Many nonprofits offer gym discounts, on-site fitness classes, or organized sports activities. This is the low-hanging fruit of fitness perks. The AHA incorporates many exercise activities at work. Employees are encouraged to take part in coaching sessions, fitness challenges, and organized and individual exercise or physical activity at work. AHA also offers onsite fitness classes in their exercise facilities and subsidized off-site gym memberships.[6]

Crisis Response Network in Tempe, Arizona, transformed an old training room into an on-site workout room after employees said they would use it to let off steam from their stressful work. The organization's health insurance carrier, Cigna, covered the cost of the equipment for the on-site gym under the organization's plan. According to Justin Chase, president, and Alexandra Zavala, VP of business operations and community integration, their organization's Employee Engagement Committee polled employees about what specific exercise equipment to purchase. The makeshift on-site gym is not only popular with staff who use it regularly, but the organization sees a significant decrease in health insurance claims.

Allyson Kapin, cofounder of Rad Campaign, which builds nonprofit websites, brings in a personal trainer to lead group workouts at the office twice a week. Says Kapin, "The staff loves it. It's a nice break from sitting or standing at the computer, keeps them more fit, and it's actually a lot of fun. Even though the workout is quite challenging, we joke around a lot and bond over the experience of doing lots of burpees. We can also get competitive with our plank time, and it's not unheard of for us to have a plank-off."

Not all nonprofit worksites are suitable for offering on-site fitness. Also, not all employees want to exercise at work; some prefer to work out in a gym or at home. The CDC offers a tool kit to help organizations identify, negotiate, and contract with fitness club providers for discounts and benefits. Many nonprofits organize group sports activities and challenges for staff that not only encourage exercise but also create a fitness-conscious community at work, building camaraderie. Staff members at GuideStar's Williamsburg, Virginia, office, for example, do laps around the walking paths in their office area together as a group.

Luz Gomez, director of research at the Knight Foundation, says staff started posting ideas on what wellness meant to them on the office's Slack channel (a mobile team communications app). Recalls Gomez, "I asked if anyone was interested in putting together a beginner's tennis class, and to my surprise, I got five people ready to do it. We had a great time. I don't know any of my coworkers that well, so it's nice to get to know them in a different setting."

Fitness challenges in the workplace are popular and easy to implement. Sharon Parkinson, senior analyst of prospect development and research at Vassar College, says, "During the fall, there's a campus-wide walking challenge for staff to form walking groups and log steps. The competition is fun, and we increase our steps every week."

Shanon Doolittle, a nonprofit consultant who worked as a staff member for a nonprofit health care organization with fitness initiatives, recalls, "For every fitness challenge we completed, we earned points. And at the end, if we had enough points, we received a discount that reduced our health care premiums during open enrollment. Each of our annual staff barbeques included a fitness activity, too, whether it was kickball, a hula-hoop contest, or volleyball. We were always intentional about adding a physical activity—other than eating."

At AHA headquarters in Dallas, in addition to the activities mentioned earlier, they have onsite walking paths. The AHA offers many useful resources and tips for organizations to integrate fitness into the workplace. One place to start is downloading the AHA's online Workplace Walking Program Kit that helps you create walking routes around the office and rewards for employees who get out of their chairs and become more active at work.

Some organizations have found that signs are simple, low cost, and effective fitness cues. The American Heart Association uses flyers and posters with advice like "Park Far, Get Ahead," to encourage employees to park their cars farther from the office and walk more. Get creative with signs to remind employees to add a little exercise into their workday.

Peter Campbell, chief information officer at Legal Services Corporation, says his HR department put up signs at the elevators encouraging employees to use the stairs. According to the CDC's online resource, "StairWELL to Better Health,"[7] using the stairs instead of going to the gym or taking a fitness class requires little additional time, no clothing change, and no additional costs. The signs Campbell's organization used are free downloads from the CDC's site.

"Our HR team is always encouraging us to be physically active, to the point where many of us hate getting caught taking the elevator," says Campbell.

One reason employees might not use the stairs could be because they perceive them as unattractive or unsafe. CDC's Division of Nutrition, Physical Activity, and Obesity conducted a study beginning in 1998 to see if making physical changes to a stairwell in the Atlanta-based Koger Center Rhodes Building, combined with music and motivational signs, would motivate employees to use the stairs. They saw an increase in employees using the enhanced stairwells for exercise.

Some nonprofits provide encouragement to staff to incorporate walking commutes or even biking, if possible. Kenny Kane, cofounder of Stupid Cancer, a nonprofit that addresses cancer in young adults, says his organization covers the cost of a CitiBike membership (a bike sharing service) for their six employees, a perk from their human resources vendor, Justworks. NTEN's Ward says that her office provides bike racks for those who bicycle to work like she does every day.

Simply implementing programs is not enough. Adding cues like signs and other reminders helps to trigger better behavior. Small and manageable investments like a crockpot in the break room or bike racks in the entryway show staff that your organization believes in and supports WE-care.

THE PHYSICAL OFFICE

We mentioned using parts of the physical office space, such as stairs and hallways, to promote well-being, but there's a lot more your organization can do to improve its environment. A physical office space is made up of everything from the art that hangs on the walls and the office floor plan to features such as standing desks, communal spaces, and a quiet room or lounge area where staff can take a break. When nonprofits invest in creating physical spaces that make employees want to show up for work, staff will be more engaged, productive, happy, and healthy. There are numerous reports, indices, and studies, such as Gensler's Workplace Index, that explore the relationship between the physical space and business performance metrics and the things employees value.

The Gensler study suggests employees need four different types of work areas to be productive to: focus, collaborate, learn, and socialize. A happy, healthy workplace is not about a fixed floor plan with designer furniture but about providing employees multiple modes of working, either alone or in groups. Experts in office design[8] say the new emphasis on employee well-being and engagement means cubicles are disappearing and being replaced by nonassigned seating, flexible and multipurpose spaces, and communal tables and workspaces. All of the latest designs try to link well-being, physical office environments, and productivity.

Take a moment to look at your nonprofit's office workspace. How does it make you feel? Do you get excited and energized or do you feel as if you are walking into a toxic wasteland? Your organization's physical office space may reflect the scarcity mentality that pervades nonprofit culture and may be perpetuating it as well.

While nonprofits may not have the budget to purchase stylish and expensive office furnishings and artwork, improving the physical office can be done inexpensively. Women's Alliance for Knowledge Exchange (WAKE), a small nonprofit that leverages technology to amplify the work of women leading change, rents a tiny office at the Tides Center in San Francisco. Its furniture is ergonomic and well designed, but it was purchased secondhand at a very low cost. The team displays beautiful photographs and artwork in the office, all provided as gifts from key partners and collaborators.

Says WAKE cofounders Trish Tierney and Heather Ramsey, "It didn't cost much to transform this office into an inspiring place to come into work every day. The key for us was to get practical pieces but also to include fun elements that bring us joy, like our curtain panels and pillows made by a friend with fabric we picked out together in Rwanda."

DonorsChoose, a nonprofit that raises money for school programs, was recognized as having one of the world's best-designed offices at World Festival of Interiors. When we saw the photos of their gorgeous space, we wondered how a nonprofit could ever afford the decor. Explains DonorsChoose's Melanie Duppins, "We secured beautiful pro-bono design work from Eight, Inc., and tens of thousands of dollars worth of donated furniture and materials, although our new office has been one of the largest structural investments we've made in our team and organization to date."

The DonorsChoose board supported this investment because:

- It provided a clean, functional, and well-designed office that would allow staff to collaborate better.
- It could help the organization attract and retain top talent.
- The staff had outgrown its previous workspace and intended to move to accommodate an anticipated increase in headcount.
- The COO was willing to execute the project and ensure it happened without a hitch.

According to Duppins, the investment has paid off. "In last year's employee survey, one of our top drivers of employee retention was the quality of relationships that existed between team members and across the organization. We believe the open layout of our office fuels these relationships and helps us preserve a culture of humility, teamwork, and transparency."

The most valuable space in the DonorsChoose office is what staff members call "the playground," a flexible space that contains lots of cozy seating and standing areas where staff can work when they need a break from their desks.

Says Duppins, "This not only helps staff climb out of the afternoon slump, it allows for impromptu problem solving and brainstorming sessions—and time to eat your lunch *away* from your desk. Both full-time and part-time staff love this space; it's part of the reason why, although many staff have the ability to work from home more often, most come in to the office to work every day."

James Siegal, CEO of KaBOOM!, an organization that helps communities design and build playgrounds, says the KaBOOM! office space is designed to bring a sense of play into the workplace.

"Our meeting rooms all feature dry-erase walls for brainstorming and holding highly interactive meetings," says Siegal. "We have a communal kitchen area—known as the KaFE—that is bustling throughout the day as staff come in and out with coffee, tea, breakfast, and lunch, and others hold scheduled or impromptu meetings at the counter space or around the café tables."

Playground components throughout their space include a tire swing in the lobby and a park bench by their front door. Other playground items are used as additional seating at individual workstations. The office has an open floor plan with most cubical walls at half-height so collaboration can take place throughout the day.

"There's a lot of natural light throughout the space, and during warmer seasons many meetings are moved outside," says Siegal. "We even have folding lawn chairs available so staff can comfortably have meetings outside on the plaza." Siegal adds that the sense of community at KaBOOM! is strong among staff and across the entire organization, supported in part by the environment, the culture, and team-building activities.

The Changing Workstation

We've talked about using standing desks and treadmill desks to stop sitting all day. Alternative desks are really valuable for productivity and mental acuity, not to mention the health benefits.

"When I returned to regular staff life, after one day of sitting, my brain felt like mud. And my butt hurt," says Gina Schmeling from Hazon, a Jewish environmental organization working to build a healthier and more sustainable Jewish community. "I ordered a Varidesk and used it for many months in the open, shared space in our offices. It was often immediately noticeable to visitors and people arriving to work if I had it up. When people were curious, I showed them how it worked, and told them how much I enjoyed it." Whenever she travels, she invites fellow staff members to log in at her computer and try it.

Your nonprofit doesn't need to break the bank to get specialized desks for all employees. Many nonprofits can afford to set up one or two standing desks for communal use. There are many inexpensive standing desk hacks using everything from cartons to music stands. There are also affordable desk toppers that mimic full standing desks. As we mentioned in Chapter 5, get an ergonomic assessment of the standing desks at your office to avoid injury and invest in soft padded mats.

Some nonprofits take workstations to a more active level by adding treadmill desks into the workplace. Desks that prompt movement can be particularly helpful at nonprofits where employees are dealing with crisis situations and susceptible to secondary trauma. In Georgia, many of the 911 call-takers in Gwinnett County tested out treadmills at their standing desks while handling calls. The program was overseen by a fitness coach with Gwinnett County's Wellness Program as part of a six-month study to document the health and stress reduction benefits.[9]

Before you install treadmill desks at your organization, encourage your staff to consult their doctors as they would before undertaking any exercise program. Check our website, www.happyhealthynonprofit.org, for more resources around movement at work.

HUMAN INTERACTIONS

In Chapter 6, we mentioned a study that found the way employees treat each other affects stress levels. We also talked about techniques individuals can use to manage their relationships in the workplace. There are also ways your organization can foster a positive work environment. This could start with implementing more stringent hiring practices, such as "the no asshole rule,"[10] to screen out potentially toxic employees. Better yet, establish compassion and kindness rituals, or even just encourage everyone to be human, to promote employee well-being.

Dennis McMillan, former executive director for the Foraker Group in Anchorage, Alaska, says, "It is hard to obtain everyone's peak performance without human connection. One option is to assure that everyone in positions of influence has personal contact with every employee, every day. How hard is it for those leaders to walk around and say hello? I guarantee it will take less time to do that than to address the issues that arise when an isolated employee burns out. Walking around, saying hello, being human, is the cheapest advice we can provide to prevent burnout."

At the Cara Program, a Chicago-based nonprofit that helps adults affected by homelessness and poverty get and keep quality jobs, stakeholders engage in a daily morning ritual that evolved organically over the organization's 25-year history. Every morning, clients, staff, and guests gather in a circle in the organization's meeting room and answer a question of the day, such as, "Who or what gives you great joy and why?" or "What has happened in your life that has motivated you to change?"

Participants share inspiring stories of personal growth and change. The morning ritual is not a visual show for donors but a chance for all to reflect on what makes everyone human. Staff and visitors alike say the experience is energizing.

"Let's face it—the work that we do is difficult," says Executive Director Maria Kim. "It's thorny and resides deep in the beauty and the mess of the human condition, and for people to thrive in this work, it requires proximity to the mission. An ability to know—in a moment, and without airs—that the work matters to real people at real inflection points in their lives. When we do this, we feel the power of the work. And on the toughest of days, that makes us feel really, really good."

Cara incorporates many other rituals to create community at work including organizing communal meals as well as taking field trips once a quarter where they tackle a topic or let off steam. They've even held a karaoke event.

"What we lacked in pitch, we certainly made up for in laughs," recalls Kim. "We also have a culture of affirmation—where we publically and periodically single out each other's contributions through a verbal high five." Cara's activities and cues encourage collegiality.

Melanie Duppins of DonorsChoose says the number one reason why their employees have long tenures working for the organization is because of their people-first culture.

"Our job in human resources is to connect [staff] with each other with simple activities. We use the 'YouEarnedIt' platform (http://youearnedit.com/) that allows staff to give each other shout-outs and accumulate points. They can redeem those points for a cash donation to one of the DonorsChoose classrooms," Melanie explains. The activity of giving gratitude is strongly aligned with the organization's mission.

Henry Timms, executive director of 92nd Street Y and cofounder of #GivingTuesday, says Rabbi Peter Rubinstein, 92Y's director of Jewish community, leads a weekly Kiddush every Friday. The rabbi's role is to oversee Jewish life at 92Y and work with staff to further the Jewish values that are the core of the organization's work. The weekly staff gathering is an opportunity to step back and connect with colleagues. Timms, who is not Jewish, says, "It provides such a simple but meaningful moment and has attracted not just Jewish colleagues but those of a range of faiths. Many look forward to it all week, just to take a chance to stop and be together. It reminded me of how powerful these kinds of rituals can be."

Timms says a group of staff started another weekly Friday event focused on fitness—not at the same time—where staff members take turns leading workouts open to everyone at the organization. They do everything from parkour and circuits to a run around Central Park. Timms reports there is a great turnout for both gatherings, and the activities add something important to the environment at 92Y, and, ultimately, to the staff's work.

Taryn Degnan, former communications staff for Common Sense Media, said staff there did something in their office they called "SURPRAISE!"

"One day, you'd walk into work, and 50 to 75 colleagues had written your praises all over Post-it notes that were stuck to your desk and computer," Degnan recalls. "It was an awesome way to have your spirits lifted and feel good about your place in the office—especially coming from many [people] you never talk to."

Traci Townsend-Gieg, a nonprofit consultant, practiced a gratitude ritual of making thank-you cards when she worked as a regional director of a health care nonprofit.

Says Townsend-Gieg, "We were on the front lines providing patient care and had so many people backing us up. So we'd do sparkly art therapy and make and sign the cards and then ship them out in the inter-office mail. It made us all feel good."

At many health care organizations, both patients and health care workers can experience stress. To address this risk, the North Hawaii Community Hospital[11] (NHCH), a 35-bed acute care hospital, created a ritual called Code Lavender, a call for support and prayer that can be initiated by patients or employees for themselves, colleagues, friends, family members, or even to be held at upcoming events.

To initiate a Code Lavender, the individual submits the date, time, and reason for the request to the hospital's holistic care services department. The recipient of the Code Lavender call must give permission for it to take place. An announcement is made, and everyone gathers in the hospital's chapel. At the chapel, the request's purpose is explained, a prayer is offered, and the recipient is presented with a prayer blanket sewn by community members and blessed by local churches. Refreshments are served and other care services such as aromatherapy and *oshibori*—a Japanese hot towel therapy—are made available.

Code Lavender reinforces the hospital's vision, mission, and spirit-centered culture of care while boosting staff morale, reducing stress and fatigue, and strengthening bonds between staff members. Think about ways your organization can implement activities and rituals, such as SURPRAISE! and Code Lavender, to support your staff.

MINDFULNESS AT WORK

As we noted in previous chapters, scientific research increasingly suggests that mindfulness not only helps employees reduce stress at work but also fosters a greater sense of well-being and increases productivity on the job. Secular mindfulness programs in the workplace are gaining popularity in the for-profit sector and could be valuable for nonprofits. Some of these programs are based on Jon Kabat-Zinn's research-tested Mindfulness-Based Stress Reduction (MBSR) program.[12] Others, referred to as "McMindfulness" by critics, aim to minimize the time involved in doing these activities using apps and online tools and shortening the practices down to 10 minutes or less a day, making them easier for people to adopt.

"Our experience has been that people are really taking to [mindfulness] as long as the leaders embody it and make it accessible instead of stuffy," says Michael Fenchel, president and COO for Breathe for Change, a nonprofit that trains educators to take care of themselves, their students, and their school communities through yoga, mindfulness, and community building.

Trish Tierney, cofounder of WAKE and former executive director of the Institute for International Education in San Francisco, recalls when one of her staff members shared a meditation practice with everyone during a staff meeting:

> As the leader, I suggested we set aside the conference room every Thursday at 11:00 A.M. and have her lead us in meditation. It was open to all. Sometimes, just a couple people showed up. Other times, it was a full room. It was not a formal organizational policy, but just something we, as an office, embraced and benefited from greatly.

Idealist, a nonprofit organization founded by Ami Dar that connects nonprofits around the world with people who want to work or volunteer for them, offers a comprehensive wellness program and employee benefits that promote well-being. Idealist has a staff member in New

York City, Caroline Contillo, who is trained as a mindfulness instructor and leads a mindfulness break at the office on a weekly basis. They use an empty conference room, arrange chairs into a circle, and guide people through the techniques. There is time for questions and comments at the end. The whole practice takes about 30 minutes.

"There are a number of reasons a regular mindfulness break can be beneficial, but one that doesn't often get mentioned is the cultivation of community," explains Contillo. "People get a sense of working on something together, even if that means just sitting in silence. Giving people the opportunity to step away from their daily routine to sit face-to-face with some colleagues in a 'circle of care' can really make the rest of the day seem doable."

Like fitness challenges, organizations can also do meditation challenges.

"We have a group of 8 to 10 of us who meditate regularly each afternoon for about 15 minutes at a time," explains Vassar College's Sharon Parkinson. "I send out [e-mails about] the Oprah/Chopra Center 21-day meditation challenges whenever those occur, and people can register for the challenge to meditate at home."

Yoga is another mindfulness practice—and physical activity—that can be brought into the workplace as an organized program. Megan Keane, membership director at NTEN, is a trained yoga instructor who has helped scores of nonprofits design and implement yoga in the workplace initiatives. She recommends that organizations identify some staff champions, especially people who are good at rallying their peers and who can build community.

"Yoga can be intimidating for anyone unfamiliar with the practice, or in a work setting, so encouragement at the beginning is key. It's also important to have a yoga teacher who is aligned with your organization's culture and values," says Keane.

Keane shares some tips for success for a yoga program in the workplace:

- **Have a dedicated space.** The space doesn't have to be fancy, and it could be as simple as pushing chairs aside in a conference room or an open space in the office with consistent availability. Providing basic yoga mats that are kept in good condition sends a message that this is a valuable offering to staff.

- **Choose an appropriate time.** Midday is often a good time for yoga in the workplace because it gives people a mindful break in the middle of their day and allows people to eat lunch afterwards.
- **Be supportive.** Getting accommodation and encouragement from management goes a long way toward sustaining a workplace yoga class.

Keane also shared that Third Sector New England has a yoga program that they've successfully had in place for several years. As a result, staff started incorporating more wellness breaks into their days and look out for one another by reminding each other to breathe or take stretch breaks. Yoga in their workplace helped them make a cultural shift toward self-care, even affecting staff who didn't attend the yoga classes.

Says Keane, "Staff came to value the class, and they covered each other's work so they could trade off attending class."

Some nonprofits offer informal yoga classes at their events or conferences. The Newark Museum created "Yoga Tuesdays" as an after-work program in the galleries, an activity proposed by staff. The event is now open to college and university students who live in the area. The program went from an informal activity to a budgeted program due to its popularity. NTEN began offering yoga and other activity sessions, such as walking and biking, at their annual conference to foster community building, networking, and mindfulness. The sessions were very well received.

Relaxation Activities

Offering meditation or yoga sessions can be relaxing for some but may not work for everyone. Another way to incorporate relaxation into the workplace is to set up a quiet room. According to Justin Chase and Alexandra Zavala at Crisis Response Network, if you simply build it, employees won't necessarily come.

"When I started, our organization had a quiet room, but it was a small room with stiff vinyl chairs, white walls, and artwork depicting close-ups of sharp cactus thorns. None of our employees used it, except to take a personal phone call during a break," Chase recalls.

The organization's Employee Engagement Committee got feedback from staff in terms of what they needed, and Chase allocated a very modest budget to transform the room. The committee ditched the chairs and brought in a comfortable couch, incandescent lamp, peaceful artwork, a sound machine that played nature sounds, painted the walls earth tones, and put blinds up on the windows.

"We wanted to create a sanctuary vibe to make it like walking into a spa," says Chase, and it worked. Staff could actually relax and decompress from their emotionally stressful work.

As we discussed in Chapter 4, there are many practices individuals can do for themselves during a stressful work day that organizations can also implement to spread chronic self-care. Massages come to mind.

"When I worked as the executive director of the local AIDS service organization, we had a generous donor whose contribution was a monthly massage for each of our four staff members," says Joy Rubey, lecturer in nonprofit management at California State University at Monterey Bay. "She [the donor] made a deal with two local massage practitioners: she paid them for 50 percent of their normal fee, and they donated the rest in kind. And it was wonderful!"

Rubey said that, at first, the massages felt like an extravagance, but they quickly became a core element of the staff's self-care program. Given the organization's limited budget, it wouldn't have been able to afford massages without the donation.

Idealist offers free monthly chair massages to staff through a partnership with a service that brings in professional massage therapists. Says Kara Montermoso, human resources manager, "These sessions are a welcome respite from desk life, provide a short but impactful mental break, and can be a good reminder that destressing and listening to one's body are important. This is an easy win both from the morale and administration side of things."

We know at this point, you might be rolling your eyes at the idea of yoga and massages at the office. But these kinds of soft perks can attract and retain top talent. The people you want working at your organization, those who can give you better results, are the people who want workplaces with happier and healthier cultures. We'll talk more about the return on investment of massages and other well-being initiatives in the workplace in Chapter 9.

CREATIVITY ACTIVITIES

We've mentioned how studies prove creativity—through painting, drawing, dancing, playing music, theater, or singing—can reduce or relieve stress. Randi Zuckerberg, in a LinkedIn post on being creative, said, "The ability to think on your toes, see things differently, notice something interesting where others see nothing, problem solve in new ways—these are all things that make a terrific employee, a great leader, and a successful entrepreneur."[13] This goes for nonprofit professionals and leaders as well.

Susie Bowie, executive director of the Manatee Community Foundation, says the organization she was with previously—Community Foundation of Sarasota County—put up a whiteboard in its break room. John Annis, senior vice president of community investment at the organization, started writing the beginning of a story on it, and staff members were encouraged to add another three to four words to it. This simple activity continued and not only built something funny or interesting for everyone to enjoy but also encouraged collaboration in a creative activity. The cues were the whiteboard and dry erase markers.

International Development Exchange (IDEX) started an artist-in-residence program to enable staff to explore vulnerability in their social justice philanthropy. A residency with accomplished interdisciplinary artists in theatrical jazz, Sharon Bridgforth and Dr. Omi Osun Joni L. Jones, offered an opportunity to explore creative processes that value mindfulness, self-awareness, improvisation, curiosity, courage, and team collaboration.

"I've been working with IDEX for 10 years, and IDEX's organizational culture and values align with my own," says Katherine Zavala, IDEX's regional director for Latin America. "And one important value is self-care—mind, body, and soul—so that I can show up authentically and be present in my work. The artists' residency was just the most the recent self-care activity for staff."

Kristine Maltrud, CEO/founder of ArtSpark, an organization that provides training for artists to develop and sustain themselves as a small business, uses many creative activities to prepare staff for teaching work. Says Maltrud, "I encourage my teachers to engage in creative or mindfulness activities within six hours of teaching a class. The activities may include going on a walk in nature and being mindful of the sights and sounds and smells, singing in the shower loudly, or doing yoga. I also have them do an exercise called 'clearing the space,' which comes from the dance world."

Creativity is a muscle that needs to be exercised like anything else. You can use organized activities or cues to encourage creativity in the workplace. Dare we say, "Get creative"?

HOME LIFE SUPPORT

Home life support includes services and programs that can help employees achieve work-life harmony such as concierge services, financial counseling, mental health counseling, employee assistance programs (EAPs), and work-life balance coaching. These programs are fairly common employee benefits, and all of them can contribute to well-being. We heard from a lot of nonprofit professionals that financial planning is particularly helpful. Often people who work at nonprofits receive low pay and experience personal financial pressures that cause imbalance.

"The lack of retirement planning, pension options, and financial literacy in nonprofits causes people a lot of stress. So people give up self-care to work more and more, some working into their 60s and 70s because saving for retirement wasn't offered," says Chari Smith, a nonprofit consultant.

Goodwill Manasota offers an array of financial education programs and services for employees with the goal of minimizing employee stress and helping employees create a strong financial plan and meet goals. Some of the programs are typical work benefits like a retirement savings and health savings accounts to cover unanticipated medical expenses. They also offer a "Goodwill Home Buyers Club," a program that prepares Goodwill team members for homeownership through education, workshops, and credit counseling. Through this club, team members can find assistance in achieving mortgage preapproval to purchase new or renovated homes, and budget coaching helps ensure successful homeownership.

Goodwill Manasota[14] also provides programs that support well-being for their team members under the umbrella of "GoodWellness." Employees are encouraged to work with a "Good Partner Coach" on work-life balance strategies. Their "GoodwillWorks" program is an employment, personal development, and training program to help employees grow personally, be successful at their careers, and achieve life goals.

Pay attention as an organization to all stakeholders. Acknowledge your employees' multifaceted lives beyond work and how that affects them at the office. The activities you offer at work to support the personal lives of your staff can pay off in the long run with less stressed and more satisfied employees.

We've just covered activities and cues that address Spheres 1, 2, and 3—Self, Others, and Environment. Now let's explore activities that transform Sphere 4, the way your organization works, and Sphere 5, how everyone uses technology.

CHAPTER 8

The Processes

Well-Being in the Workplace

So far, everything's working with our walking meetings except the whiteboard.

WORKFLOWS

There is no single right way to work, but there are many ways to work badly, and almost all of them can be avoided. Laying out specific ground rules for how and when to work and how and when not to work is a start to managing your organization's workflows. For example, constant interruptions from e-mails, phone calls, and office drop-ins can be disruptive to focus and stressful. Supporting work processes that protect staff from unnecessary intrusions in their workday can relieve that stress.

Kat Morgan, a consultant who has worked in social service nonprofits, worked for one organization where staff members were encouraged to block out chunks of time in their calendars to focus on projects such as report writing, planning, follow-up, and curriculum development. "[We] had explicit support and permission to only answer e-mail during specific times each day. There was an expectation that appointments were the preferred way to discuss things with colleagues and interrupting each other by dropping by was discouraged."

The way work tasks are assigned to staff can also create stress, but that, too, can be addressed. When Morgan worked for a shelter, the hotline—a program of a larger agency—was run by only a handful of shelter staff. Morgan expanded the hotline to make it a responsibility of all agency staff:

> Once it became a shared responsibility, staff were then able to focus on the hotline when they covered it and didn't have to simultaneously meet with clients, call case managers, and do other work. It also had the added benefit of breaking some of the existing silos. It fostered a sense of team and became a professional development opportunity for nonshelter staff.

Morgan says since more staff engaged in services delivery by covering the hotline, quality improvement occurred. Eventually, nearly all staff covered at least one hotline shift each week:

> The hotline went from being perceived as a dreadful burden handled by only a few resentful staff—those at highest risk for burnout—to being treated as a core service by the whole agency. In addition, every staff member became a stronger ambassador for the organization and advocate for our clients. Finally, it made scheduling vacations and managing sick days much less

challenging and less burdensome for the staff who served as backup—typically the management team.

ENERGY MANAGEMENT

In Chapter 5, we explained how experts say your brain focuses for 90 to 120 minutes before you need a break for 10 to 20 minutes due to ultradian rhythms. To manage everyone's energy at your nonprofit, you need to identify peak production times for your entire staff. Then you need to organize workflow to capitalize on optimal times.

Timothy Fowler, STEM coordinator at AmeriCorps VISTA for AfterSchool Works! New York, described how his organization did just that. The organization's deputy director, Alli Lidie, asked all six staff members to track their work and time across a week to help identify when they felt productive versus unproductive.

Says Fowler, "The goal was to identify those times of day when we get the most done, and capitalize on it, but also not interrupt each other during a productive time. So it had personal and team components to it."

Senior leadership initiated the study and helped staff interpret and apply the results. The resulting data was used to show staff the best times to schedule group calls and other meetings such as later in the day when they might otherwise be unproductive.

Energy management techniques such as Peter Bregman's "18 Minutes a Day" technique can be incorporated throughout your organization. Have staff think of and write down three important things they want to accomplish in the day for five minutes in the morning or do this in an e-mail or at a brief staff gathering. Set an alarm that everyone can hear that beeps or rings every hour. Each time it does, instruct staff to quickly review if they are on track. At the end of the day, prompt staff to ask themselves what they did and didn't accomplish and contemplate why. Turning solo practices into group practices can promote better work habits and teamwork.

WALKING AS WORK

Many workplaces consider walking a break activity instead of a part of the actual work. Walking provides many work-related benefits beyond fitness and energy boosting including creativity, leadership development, and relationship building. Karen Bloom, chief advancement officer for Project Kesher, an organization that trains women to become change-makers with leadership programs based on Jewish identity building and social activism, realized staff behavior needed to reflect the changes they were trying to make in the world.

At Project Kesher, Bloom uses the restorative qualities of a walk in the woods to be more productive. Project Kesher is located in a large, shared office building in New York's Westchester County next to a county park with beautiful hiking trails. Bloom takes solitary hikes and walks as often as she can to refresh herself. She also leads regular "walk and talks" with staff, in small groups and one-on-ones.

Says Bloom, "If we are sitting in a staff meeting and trying to tackle a problem, I get them to stop, and I say, 'let's put this on our hiking meeting agenda.' We will go in the woods with our list and brainstorm ideas for campaigns or programs. We have found that a one-hour walking brainstorm yields more creative ideas than if we sit in our chairs in a stuffy conference room."[1]

Bloom takes walking as work seriously and conducts one-on-one walking meetings with major donors, getting to the business at hand and building relationships walking shoulder-to-shoulder with them. She also leads a monthly walk for staff at other companies and organizations in their office building. She does this rain or shine, even in the snow. She has even used walking to help raise money for her organization by offering a walk and talk as a fund-raising auction item. Because Bloom is a senior leader who practices what her organization preaches in terms of self-care, she makes good behavior contagious.

Gina Schmeling, director of individual giving at Hazon, says inspiring her colleagues to walk and stand was made easier by Hazon's organizational culture.

"We strive to make ourselves happy and healthy as well as the communities we support," Schmeling explains.

Each week, Schmeling e-mails staff to say the "weekly afternoon walk," or WAW, is on and promotes it using social media and adding it as a Google calendar entry on the organization's shared calendar. In the beginning, only one staffer joined her. A few weeks later, there were two and then three.

"All of a sudden we had 12 walkers," says Schmeling. "Each week, we did the same walk: to the East River, down to South Ferry, back to the office. I kept strict time on my watch, making sure everyone was back at the office in 20 minutes. I wanted to earn the trust of managers and allow staff to plan their days."

Schmeling takes a selfie of the group to document every walk and generate additional interest. "My ideas and strategies about movement took root easily, and already more of my coworkers are thinking up new ways to move at work."

Erin Kelly, social media manager at the Robert Wood Johnson Foundation, says the foundation gives employees the autonomy to take movement breaks and to find an activity that suits them, whether that means a walk on a trail or a class in the fitness center. The foundation employs a full-time wellness staff person who cultivates interest and engagement in staff to help them maintain healthy lifestyles.

Says Kelly, "From a 10-minute walk when the spring sun shines to helping a meeting planner incorporate activity breaks into a day-long agenda, these are just a few of the many ways we incorporate movement into work."

Heidi Simon, communications and public affairs manager for America Walks, a national organization that works to provide every community with safe and accessible walking conditions, notes, "When we talk 'walking meetings,' we need to incorporate walkability, rollability, and all forms of mobility. This means planning and preparation to ensure routes that are enjoyable and accessible for all participants."

Check out resources for walking meetings at www.americawalks.org.

Walking Meeting Tips

A big part of working for a nonprofit is attending meetings. There are many different types of meetings for nonprofit professionals including one-on-one check-ins, small team meetings, large team meetings, department meetings, and all-staff meetings. There are also virtual meetings, conference calls, online chats, and webinars.

The following are tasks and activities perfect for walking meetings:

- Educate and inform
- Problem solve
- Enhance creativity
- Socialize and build team spirit
- Make decisions
- Resolve conflict

Walking removes the barriers of a desk and chair, and lets people communicate more equally. Start with the one-on-one check-in meeting with a direct report or your boss. Meeting and walking as a pair tends to be easier. Walk for the bulk of the meeting, then return to the office for the last five minutes to document any notes or to-dos. Suggest replacing weekly status updates with supervisors with a walking meeting and build up to more frequent strolls.

If it isn't feasible to walk outside due to weather, map out walking trails in your building, and do the meeting inside. You can also move chairs away and lead a standing meeting where everyone stands for 15 to 30 minutes. Standing meetings are suitable for check-ins on projects. If your staff spends a lot of time on conference calls, suggest that employees forward calls to their mobile phone and pace or walk around instead of sitting at their desks. If you're having a brainstorming meeting, make it even more productive by making it a walking meeting. Walk to change up the dynamics of a small group meeting. Strive to hold a few walking meetings each week.

Always give enough warning for a walking meeting so people can dress accordingly—bring a coat or sweater and wear comfortable shoes. Walking meetings in high heels are not much fun. Suggest that workers wear comfortable shoes to work or keep a pair at their desk for impromptu walking meetings. Also remind participants to bring their water bottles, phones, or pens and notebooks for note taking.

As with any meeting, facilitators should still send out a formal agenda to keep everyone on track, but there are also some other things you need to think about. You need to allow time for stretching and breaks. Also, allow time to capture notes after the meeting. Some nonprofit professionals recommend using a pen and small pad to jot down notes as you go or use your phone to take audio notes. You'll be pleasantly surprised how you'll retain information better from walking meetings and need only a few quiet minutes when you get back to write and capture ideas. Meetings that require technology and an Internet connection can easily be transferred to a mobile phone while you walk.

If possible, plan your route in advance so you know how far you can walk in your allotted time and avoid noisy spots or too-narrow walkways. Plot out a few walking routes that work out to the typical length of staff meetings. Consider paths that take 15, 30, and 60 minutes to complete. Use a park or pleasant outdoor setting whenever possible. Keep in mind the walkability issues if your walking meeting includes staff with walking challenges or in wheelchairs. Try scheduling walking meetings in the afternoon when employees' energy levels are lowest—the fresh air will revive them.

Encourage everyone to track steps with a Fitbit or other wearable device. You'll be amazed to see how much additional physical activity everyone gets by having a few walking meetings a week. You can simultaneously run a step challenge using Fitbit or other tracking apps to encourage healthy competition.

Walking the Actual Walk

If you have more than one other person with you, you will have to use a little choreography to have a productive walking meeting. Remember to be inclusive when you have staff with walking limitations. The rule for walking meetings is: slowest walker sets the pace. Here are things to consider depending on the size of your group.

Group meetings of 3–5: Consider the width of the sidewalk or path, variations in terrain, and possible physical barriers. This group size is flexible, and discussion can occur while walking, or if desired, the group can stop along the walk.

Groups of 6–15: With larger groups, participants will likely need to deal with multiple side conversations that are fine for brainstorming or problem solving, but they need to stop and regroup to keep the meeting productive. America Walks plans larger team walking meetings so there is a stop in a coffee shop and arranges for an intern to meet them with a laptop in case they need to reference some information. Plan a route with some good stopping points.

Groups larger than 15: Big groups tend to require more planning with a strong leader and potentially a few assistants, as needed. There will be conversations while walking, then planned stops for presentations. When you start out, tell people that you are walking for work and community, not fitness—so remind them that the slowest walker sets the pace.

Establish ground rules such as "stay with the group" before you head out. If you have a larger group, you might want to designate someone as the note taker or break people up into smaller groups with designated discussion leaders. You can also break the group up by their walking pace. Include group stops in your meeting to summarize agenda points and shift into next topic.

Getting more movement into the workday and looking at movement as an integral part of work can give your staff more energy and vitality. But sometimes what everyone needs is more flexibility to deal with their multifaceted lives and be better able to focus on their work. Energy management is great for staff well-being, but flexibility can be even better.

FLEXIBLE WORK

According to the website When Work Works,[2] a joint project of the Families and Work Institute (FWI) and the Society for Human Resource Management (SHRM), flexible work is about improving business results by giving people more control over their work time and schedules. Nonprofits have experimented with a variety of approaches to flexible work that include flexible hours and flexible locations such as working from home, virtual offices, self-scheduling, shift trading, and telecommuting. To be successful, flexible work requires supportive managers and the assurance of no job jeopardy if an individual chooses the option to work flexibly.

In Chapter 9, we'll discuss the policies around flexible work, but here are some examples of flexible work models:

Results-Only Work Environment

A Results-Only Work Environment (ROWE)[3] is considered the ultimate flexible work model "where employees can do whatever they want whenever they want, as long as the work gets done." This means that the organization sets no standard hours and no mandatory (and time wasting) meetings and doesn't require staff to get permission to take personal time to attend a family event. While this process may sound surreal, it is a workplace method based on the popular book *Why Work Sucks and How to Fix It: The Results-Only Revolution* by Cali Ressler and Jody Thompson. Advocates claim that ROWE not only makes employees happier but also delivers better results.

The Minnesota Council on Foundations (MCF) began its evolution to ROWE in late 2013. A catalyst for the change was the arrival of a new president, Trista Harris. Harris says the organization decided it made more sense to "treat staff like adults and reward them for what they accomplished, rather than for the time they spent sitting at their desks."

The staff formed three-person book clubs to discuss Ressler and Thompson's book, how best to implement ROWE at their organization, questions about ROWE ideas, and what parts of their current culture would be problematic in a ROWE workplace.

Says Harris, "Ideas that came out of the book clubs included that MCF and each staff person needed clear and measureable goals. Staff needed to be better communicators and have more trust that coworkers would do as they had promised. In addition, we determined that our work groups had to function better as true teams."

Everyone in the organization shifted focus away from what it looked like someone was doing to what someone was actually accomplishing. In the organization's annual 360-degree review where all staff and board members weigh in, ROWE comes up every year with positive comments.

Four-Day Workweek

The four-day workweek is exactly that: staff work four days each week but for longer hours. In return, they get three-day weekends.

Rockwood Leadership Institute teaches nonprofit and social justice leaders something called "personal ecology," a concept developed at Oxford University in the 1920s. On its website, Rockwood Leadership refers to personal ecology as "maintaining balance, pacing, and efficiency to sustain your energy over a lifetime of activism." Since 2008, Rockwood supports its staff's personal ecology by instituting a four-day, 32-hour workweek. Staff gets time to explore outside interests and run personal errands while still completing their work.

Not only does a shorter workweek give staff the chance to replenish their energy, it also strengthens the organization. Staff say they feel fully rested and energized on Mondays so they are more efficient when they are at work. They experience improved ability to prioritize, schedule, and manage their time as well as better team interpersonal dynamics. Staff reported feeling more joy in their work and less burnout.

To be fair, they did experience some downsides. Staff reported challenges with answering the e-mail that builds up over the three-day weekend and with creating efficient systems to get work done in a timely manner. Some staff also felt guilt about "not doing enough."[4] There is no magic bullet solution to all work and workplace dynamics. Always weigh benefits against any possible downsides.

Flextime can have a positive effect on staff, but so can flex space, working virtually, and leveraging virtual workplaces because of the Internet. MomsRising is run by a small staff working virtually from their home offices around the country. The virtual nature of their organization offers flexibility without compromising staff productivity.

"Having a flexible workplace arrangement is so useful in both my work *and* personal life," says Anita Jackson, director of social media strategy at MomsRising. "It means that when the school calls me because my kid is sick, I can go pick her up without worrying about 'leaving the office.' Put another way, it means there's no judgment in the workplace when the inevitable overlap with the rest of life happens. Eliminating that source of worry in the workplace also eliminates resentment about the workplace. And avoiding resentment about one's place of work really helps avoid burnout."

At MomsRising, a virtual workplace doesn't mean zero accountability. Staff is expected to be available during normal business working hours and deliver on their work tasks. But as Jackson points out, "A results-oriented workplace means that there's little to no time spent in the workplace just to appear busy. We do have an expectation of a 40-hour workweek for full-time employees, but if you work late one evening and then go to a yoga class during the next day, that's respected as your choice. And that in itself is revitalizing—to have the freedom to make choices that best serve the work and your humanity."

PLAY AT WORK

Organizations with flexible work don't see it as goofing off or shirking work responsibilities. We're now going to tell you that everyone should play at work. Yes, play. According to Boston College developmental psychologist Peter Gray, play helped early humans cooperate, share, and exist in relative peace. Today, social play—even with adults—"counteracts tendencies toward greed and arrogance and promotes concern for the feelings and well-being of others."[5]

In an interview in *Pacific Standard*, psychologist Kathryn Hirsh-Pasek, author of *Why They Need to Play More and Memorize Less*, says there are three main attributes of play:[6]

1. Voluntary—you aren't obligated to do it.
2. Flexible—it's changeable.
3. Enjoyable and fun—and it builds imagination.

Play has a positive impact on humans no matter their age; however, play has also gotten the short end of the stick, treated as childish or frivolous and abandoned after people grow up. According to research compiled by business software consulting firm TechnologyAdvice, playing games—or gamification—affects the brain positively by increasing motivation, improving memory, increasing efficiency, and even enhancing feelings of empathy. Play not only reduces stress in the workplace, but also enhances the work environment, and improves the quality of work.

James Siegal, CEO of KaBOOM!, an organization with a mission to bring play to children, agrees that play is very important for adults in the workplace:

> We've found that by encouraging routinely scheduled play breaks, as well as impromptu breaks, KaBOOM! staff—aka Boomers—are able to recharge, refocus, and deliver higher quality work.

KaBOOM! employees engage in many types of play activities, from playing Bananagrams to an outdoor game like kickball. Says Siegal, "Just one hour away from typical workday business results in reenergized staff and more creative problem solving."

For Susan Edwards, associate director for digital content at Hammer Museum, the act of making games is a form of play for her. She then brings some of those games to her workplace. Edwards says there are many benefits to game-playing at work, including improved camaraderie and collaboration because personal connections are made and collaboration is practiced in a nonthreatening low-stakes environment.

Says Edwards, "For me, it's also about just having fun and providing some stress relief from the workday."

Edwards points out that sometimes it is a challenge to get work colleagues to view playing games as doing work. "I find that you have to get people to just try it the first time. Once they see the benefits to having a lot of fun, they are hooked."

Edwards offers some simple advice to getting started: If you want to integrate playful techniques into actual work, start with projects that aren't high-stakes. Start with simple games with only one or two rules or games everyone already knows how to play. Try to match the games to specific challenges your team is facing.

Rachel Piontak, program administrator at American Indian College Fund, says her organization uses a variety of fun activities at its retreats that tend to center around food and shared experiences.

"Like many small teams, we initially tried traditional icebreakers but found many of them unsuited for our team's sharing and warm-up style," explains Piontak. "We realized that we enjoy time together eating, specifically a potluck style with homemade dishes, and reflecting on our initiatives, obstacles, and life in general through shared experiences. Our fun is found in storytelling and creating memories together at our retreats. When we're not enjoying a good meal, our team explores museums or other activities that allow us a space to reflect and explore."

Another nonprofit professional, Teresa Crawford, executive director of the Social Sector Accelerator at Counterpart International, recalls, "When I worked for Partners Global, we used play in our conferences, meetings, and retreats. We've used Legos, Play-Doh, sing-alongs, cookie decorating, and more."

Surfrider Foundation, a network of surfers who want to protect the ocean, has a ping-pong table and dartboards in their break room. They also host daily "board meetings," literally lunchtime surf sessions. Get it? As with any play activities and cues for well-being, we encourage you to look at a diverse selection of play options and incorporate both scheduled and random play into everyone's workdays and workweeks.

BREAKING FROM WORK

We've talked about the importance of flextime and playtime at work, but sometimes staff just needs a break to be more productive. Closing the office early, encouraging people to leave right at closing time, or designating specific times of day for group breaks can reduce stress and contribute to employee well-being. Encouraging employees to take minibreaks during the workday, even just to get up to stretch or walk around the office, can be like rebooting a computer.

"Our team regularly breaks around 2:00 in the afternoon to do a 10-minute workout," says Bridgett Colling from the marketing agency See3. "We find workouts on YouTube or Pinterest and do them as a group using yoga mats we keep in the office. Taking some time to step away from my desk and get my blood pumping usually gives me a much greater energy boost than another cup of coffee or something filled with sugar."

Here are some more ideas for breaks from nonprofits:

- Mervyn Humphreys, a manager at the Child Migrants Trust, a charity that helps families separated by forced migration, says their HR strategy tries to build in work-life balance. Staff finishes at 3:30 P.M. on Fridays and everyone has the day off on their birthdays.[7]
- The World Wildlife Fund gives its entire team a day off every other Friday. Dubbed "Panda Fridays," this biweekly break furnishes staff with downtime so they can spend more quality time with their families or pursue outside interests.[8]
- Remember Do Something's Toto Tuesdays where employees were forced out of the office on time on Tuesdays by playing Toto's song "Africa" loudly until they left? That's a fun and creative way to encourage breaking from work.[9]

Providing even small organized and accepted breaks in the day and workweek can give employees the space they need to replenish their energy and better manage work and life responsibilities.

Real Vacations

There is another way that your organization can encourage people to break from work. It's called a vacation. A *real* vacation. Your organization should encourage employees to take time off, and this should come from the top. When vacations are not mandated, there is often a disconnection between what is written in an organization's employee handbook about vacation time and what actually happens. Vacations supported by policies and organization leaders help individuals set and keep boundaries.

Dennis McMillan, former executive director of the Foraker Group, admits that the staff there worked long hours, but management tried to offset that, urging—even demanding—employees take time off.

"A few years ago, we had a problem, even with our Gen X and younger staff, with people working too many hours," McMillan recalls. "We put them on a 'diet plan.' We made everyone count hours, like calories, and start reducing their excess time."

Vacations should become cultural norms within your organization and not be frowned upon as shirking work or be subliminally discouraged. Being supportive of vacation time means not imposing work deliverables during employees' vacations and not contacting them or expecting them to respond or contact the office.

Says consultant Kat Morgan, "As a supervisor, I always see a core part of my supervisory role is to encourage staff to keep healthy boundaries with their jobs. This means not calling them when they are on vacation."

Organizations can monitor and be aware of when employees are not taking their vacation time and provide positive feedback to encourage them to do so. Ignoring vacation benefits should not be a badge of honor, just like lack of sleep shouldn't.

Melanie Duppins, of DonorsChoose, says, "We offer 25 days a year of paid vacation and track vacation usage. We work with managers to encourage their staff to take their vacation time. We let the manager customize the message to the specific situation. For example, we might have a workaholic type where the manager needs to insist that they take vacation, or maybe it is about us problem-solving with the manager to adjust the workload so the employee can take off. Or sometimes we might have people burning the midnight oil for days in row, and we talk to the manager about offering comp time."

Many nonprofits are starting to offer additional time off for self-care. Mind, a nonprofit in the United Kingdom that provides mental health services, encourages employees to work with their managers to identify specific self-care needs. That led to what the organization calls "mind days," an extra six days of holiday per year for employees.[10]

When possible, close your organization's offices during holidays to make it impossible for people to come into work. Foster a culture of respecting work-life boundaries and allowing staff downtime during symbolically important events.

Sabbaticals

Sometimes, people need a more extended break beyond a mental health day or real vacation. That's where sabbaticals come in. A sabbatical is a period of time during which someone does not work at his or her regular job and is able to rest, travel, or do research. Sabbaticals are being adopted more widely by nonprofits as an integral way to support leaders and staff to prevent burnout.

In 2009, Alaska's largest family foundation, the Rasmuson Foundation, conducted a collective study of the results of sabbatical programs called *Creative Disruption: Sabbaticals for Capacity Building & Leadership Development in the Nonprofit Sector* along with the Barr Foundation (Boston), The Durfee Foundation (Los Angeles), the Virginia G. Piper Charitable Trust (Phoenix), and Alston/Bannerman Fellowship Program (national). The authors of the study, Deborah S. Linnell of Third Sector New England and Tim Wolfred, PsyD, of CompassPoint Nonprofit Services, discovered that the majority of nonprofit leaders who took sabbaticals experienced improved work-life balance, improved family connections, and better physical health. They also experienced dramatic organizational effectiveness upon returning to their jobs.[11]

Since 2009, the Rasmuson Foundation has been providing funding and planning assistance for sabbaticals for nonprofit leaders from two to six months in duration. Dennis McMillan was involved in the study and reported that many nonprofit leaders in Alaska who took sabbaticals found the time away helped them and their boards and staff gain a new perspective about their work. McMillan's organization later received the sabbatical grant allowing him to take a sabbatical of his own.

"The board and staff functioned at full capacity during my absence. No one needed to contact me. Everything stayed on track, including preparing for our annual meeting the week I returned. No surprise, everything was expected to be okay and it was," McMillan wrote in a post online. He said he provided a "cardboard Dennis" to display at the office "to help with visual separation."

McMillan continued, "Since the board's objectives were to get away, stay out of touch and relax, I feel that I was able to accomplish what they expected. I did not call work. Work did not call me. I spent quality time with relatives—many of whom I have rarely seen while living in Alaska. I also reinforced an insight I had prior to the sabbatical that I needed to be more disciplined about taking time for me. After the sabbatical, I committed that discipline would be continued."[12]

Mari Kuraishi, cofounder and president of GlobalGiving, who took a sabbatical from her organization, says that the sabbatical served several purposes:

> First, it proved to the team here, as well as our board, that we have an awesome team that delivers amazing results with or without me. That's probably the most important thing—it's proof of organizational health. Second, it gave me an opportunity to recharge and to see things in a different perspective. It was the first time in decades I'd not had a long to-do list and a packed schedule.

Kuraishi says the sabbatical was like a reboot, and she learned some key life lessons and came back to the workplace with a fundamentally different perspective.

Nina Stack, president of the Council of New Jersey Grantmakers, took a sabbatical and shares her take on them:

> Many years ago I made the choice to spend my career working for and in organizations that were about improving the lives of others. This is incredibly rewarding work emotionally. But nonprofit work can take a toll mentally and physically, often because the organizations are scrambling for money. As the tasks mount and responsibilities build, there is less and less time for self-care let alone "blue sky" or "outside the box imagining' that could benefit the organization and the people and communities it serves. I'm enormously grateful to have had this time for reflection, creativity, and dreaming.[13]

Nancy Schwartz, a well-respected nonprofit marketing problem solver and coach at GettingAttention.org, took a sabbatical for two months. Beyond the physical, emotional, and intellectual recharge, she says, "As a driven person, jumping fully off the treadmill via my sabbatical was the *only way* to gain the perspective I needed to see what was next for my professional life. I had been trying to see that for years but was as overwhelmed by the day-to-day as everyone else. When I did return to work after a two-month break, I focused on bringing my new professional vision to life."

Both Do Something and Crisis Text Line offer sabbaticals to staff members who have been at their respective organizations for two years. Staff is encouraged to take a month off to volunteer anywhere in the world with a commitment to return for a third year with the organization. Says Aria Finger, Do Something CEO, "Sabbaticals are a really excellent way to prevent or recover from burnout. A sabbatical program is also a retention piece."

Sarah Durham, president of Big Duck, a communications firm that works with nonprofits, took a sabbatical after 20 years on the job:

> Stepping away from your job gives everyone perspective. For me, it was a reset moment. I came back with a clear sense of the work I was eager to pick up again and what I hoped I could let go of permanently. My job description was completely rewritten because I realized what I should and shouldn't be doing at work and what others could do more effectively. Even today, over a year later, my job is still the "new" job, not the old job.

Durham goes on to say that for her colleagues, her sabbatical was a chance to try new things, experiment, and take on new responsibilities. Several people stepped up and became leaders, and that positive outcome has endured.

Says Durham, "Best of all, everyone felt good about the ability of the 'machine' to run without any one person being totally indispensable, which seems very healthy, too. It took pressure off me and redistributed it with more balance than we'd had before."

Define the parameters of a sabbatical program at your organization and how it will benefit your organization as a whole. Sabbaticals require planning so they aren't unduly disruptive to the organization, and they might require policy changes. Clearly from the stories we've heard, sabbaticals are beneficial for both individuals and the organizations where they work.

Digital Detoxes

Tech breaks—or digital detoxes—can be organization-wide activities to reduce staff stress and pressure. Going off-line for a couple of hours or days and setting limits on tech use, both at and away from work, can support tech wellness. Unhealthy attitudes toward digital communications at your nonprofit can be managed by carefully crafted and communicated e-mail etiquette guidelines.

Annelisa Stephan, manager for digital engagement at J. Paul Getty Trust, is interested in the importance of an organization's "rhythm" that can perpetuate inefficiencies. "E-mail can be a venue for the martyr complex to be played out: whoever sends the most e-mails late at night or on a Sunday, is the most dedicated worker," says Stephan. Not the kind of relationship to tech you want to perpetuate.

At the David and Lucile Packard Foundation, the Organizational Effectiveness and Philanthropy team has articulated that they don't expect responses to e-mails over the weekend and that if someone is included in the cc: line, they don't have to respond at all. Kathy Reich, director of the program, says they have an actual rule about not sending any e-mails in the evenings or on weekends.

"The bottom line is that, even in the busiest workplace, we need to schedule quiet time. It is as important as that urgent e-mail we think we must answer *now*," wrote Dennis McMillan in a blog post.[14] Those quiet times can be designated technology-free times or involve activities that cultivate technology wellness.

Digital detoxes have been popularized in recent years by events such as the National Day of Unplugging that we mentioned in Chapter 5. The nationwide event begins at sundown on the first Friday in March and ends at sundown on Saturday. Turn this day into an organization-wide event by encouraging staff to take the National Day of Unplugging pledge and to completely disconnect for the 24-hour period. Make it an annual tradition or, better yet, build on it and make it a monthly ritual or even weekly for staff to participate together and reap the benefits of disconnecting with intention.

Getting off digital technology for a while doesn't mean ripping out the Internet cables, shutting down Wi-Fi, and having staff use smoke signals to communicate. Kopernik, a nonprofit organization that brings technology to the developing world, practices digital detoxes in its workplace. Sally Bolton, the organization's communications manager, shared some ways they cut down on employee's digital stress:

- Encourage good e-mail communications guidelines such as brevity, clear asks, and clear subject lines.
- Set up internal chat lines for sharing photos or brief social updates.
- Encourage staff to stay off of e-mail during the weekends or after hours.
- Use retreats as a time for digital detox—stay off e-mail and devices during the retreat meeting.

In the last two chapters, we've presented you with a buffet of effective happy, healthy activities and cues. If implemented haphazardly, your efforts are not going to be effective. Getting input from employees is essential. Securing leadership buy-in is important as well. Design workplace well-being activities that support the individuals working hard on your organization's mission while serving others. Now it's time to pull together your organization-wide programs and well-being efforts into a Happy, Healthy Strategy.

CHAPTER 9

The Strategy

Working toward a Happy, Healthy Nonprofit Organization

Clearly there's some nuance to this "relieving stress by bringing dogs to the office" thing that we're missing.

WELLNESS VERSUS WELL-BEING PROGRAMS

Strategies that promote well-being in the workplace complement any traditional wellness programs or employee benefits you might already offer. Your Happy, Healthy Strategy covers the multiple facets of your employees' lives and your organization's culture. Your Happy, Healthy Strategy of well-being is much broader than a traditional wellness program and can draw from or enhance other types of internal plans.

The Kaiser Family Foundation's annual survey of trends in employer-sponsored health coverage, benefits, and programs defines wellness programs as *efforts to improve health and lower costs*. The survey found that "a majority of large employers now offer health screening programs including health risk assessments, questionnaires asking employees about lifestyle, stress, or physical health, and biometric screening." The survey defines these assessments as "in-person health examinations conducted by a medical professional."[1]

The Rand Corporation's *Workplace Wellness Programs Study: Final Report, 2013* describes the traditional workplace wellness program model and how it is delivered and evaluated. According to the report, workplace wellness programs include "wellness screening activities to identify health risks and interventions to reduce risks and promote healthy lifestyles."[2]

A Happy, Healthy Strategy takes on the wider lens of well-being in the workplace where physical health is just one aspect. Think of the Five Spheres of Happy, Healthy Living as a framework. Well-being affects more than just our physical self, but also our relationship to others, the environment, work, and technology—a 360-degree scope. A Happy, Healthy Strategy increases the effectiveness of workplace wellness programs and creates a deeper cultural shift with more sustainable change. A Happy, Healthy Strategy engages your leadership and staff in a collaborative effort to improve the well-being of each individual and your organization as a whole.

Amber Hacker, vice president of operations at Interfaith Youth Core, says her organization takes a holistic approach to well-being, starting with its core organizational value: renewal. "This theme is something that informs our talent development strategy, our health and work benefits and policies, and workplace activities. We want to ensure meaningful careers for our staff who stay with us long term and avoid burnout. For example, we offer a benefit of allowing employees to have flexible schedules, like leaving the office early one day if they are taking a graduate class. The activity falls into self-care but supports employee well-being and is connected to our values."

Melanie Duppins, VP of human capital and teacher outreach at DonorsChoose, says, "We care about our employees' well-being, and it is much more organic than the traditional wellness program offerings that we also provide. Any time we consider launching activities, we benchmark them against the Gallup Five Elements of Wellbeing: career, social, financial, physical, and community."[3]

Duppins' organization also gets feedback from staff because if it doesn't "have roots in what they really want and isn't meaningful to them," they are wasting everyone's time.

"We create the space to empower staff to drive it," says Duppins. "Our strategy is a set of initiatives that are easy to adopt and nimble. We want to live our values about well-being in the workplace, not provide activities where no one engages."

The CEO of USA for UNHCR (United Nations High Commissioner for Refugees) has strong opinions about how some organizations approach their wellness programs.

"I am somewhat appalled how some workplaces carry it out," says Anne-Marie Grey, executive director and CEO. "When the emphasis is purely on reducing health costs and tracking employees' healthy—and not so healthy—behaviors at the individual level, I am not a fan."

Grey reports that her organization focused on the theme of work-life balance and made a policy of no e-mails except for emergencies between 6:00 P.M. and 6:00 A.M. on weekdays and never on weekends. They also do not schedule meetings before 10:00 A.M. or after 3:00 P.M., allowing for time for staff to organize, plan, and do real work. They addressed nutrition in the workplace by removing the vending machines, fake creamers, and sodas and replaced them with water, good coffee, and health bars. They instituted a policy giving all employees 40 hours of paid volunteer time, whether they coached a Little League team, took mission trips, or did whatever else interested them.

Your Happy, Healthy Strategy ties passion for your organization's mission to personal well-being. Taking care of your staff doesn't mean a failure to take care of those being served by your organization. In contrast, nourishing from within means more energy, attention, and drive for the challenging, important work that many nonprofits do every day.

THE BENEFITS OF A HAPPY, HEALTHY STRATEGY

Carefully designed and implemented traditional wellness programs and well-being initiatives can reduce health care costs. The Humane Society of the United States encourages its employees to participate in educational wellness webinars. In return, employees get discounts on their health insurance premium monthly fees. The Crisis Response Network in Tempe, Arizona, saved on the cost of purchasing gym and workout equipment because its health care insurance carrier covered the cost. These savings can be positive outcomes for any organization with well-organized and utilized wellness and well-being programs.

Katie Delahaye (KD) Paine, CEO of Paine Publishing and measurement expert, notes that more than a decade ago, research tied engaged employees directly to improved customer service and higher profits. Paine says, "Today, when your employees aren't just the face of your nonprofit but your brand ambassadors in their neighborhoods and in social networks, it is critical to keep them healthy, happy, and engaged. The payoff is huge, with lower recruitment costs, higher retention, and more efficiency."

Wellness and well-being activities translate into increased effectiveness and productivity and can be directly mapped to results in your organization's logic models. These include:

- Higher employee work satisfaction and retention
- Ability to attract top talent when recruiting for jobs
- Higher productivity
- Greater ability to handle stressful situations
- Ability to meet and exceed milestones
- Motivated, resilient workers
- Better brand ambassadors
- Responsive and engaged staff
- Fewer absences and sick days

A Happy, Healthy Nonprofit that incorporates self-care and well-being into the way it works can reap tangible rewards.

Six Steps to Getting Started

Your Happy, Healthy Strategy spells out how you'll bring self-care into the workplace as a part of everyone's work and outlines the benefits you anticipate as a result. Becoming happy and healthy takes a long-term commitment to change what isn't working within your organization and seek happier, healthier alternatives that help your nonprofit better achieve its mission. Once you've taken an honest and thorough assessment of your organization's culture (see Chapter 6), you need to implement the following six things to move your Happy, Healthy Strategy forward:

1. Get leadership buy-in.
2. Use internal champions.
3. Establish an employee engagement committee.
4. Get feedback and gauge needs.
5. Work with partners and resources.
6. Establish a budget.

Let's take a more detailed look at these action items.

Step 1: Get leadership buy-in. If you're on staff, buy-in might start with your executive director. If you're the ED, this means getting board buy-in but also getting buy-in from staff. Prepare a presentation for your board that focuses on benefits including increased productivity, boosted employee morale, and stronger staff retention.

Step 2: Identify in-house champions. There are people within your organization who are already engaging in self-care behaviors or working to develop better self-care habits. If you're the champion of happy healthy in your organization, identify others and enlist their support. Turn small happy, healthy behaviors of a few into contagions to infect your organization with the well-being bug.

Step 3: Establish an employee engagement committee. Assemble a formal standing committee of employees who will serve as your advisers on what well-being programs and activities to design, test, launch, and iterate.

Step 4: Feedback and gauging needs. Your Happy, Healthy Committee should spearhead an internal effort to gather feedback from staff. They can survey your staff anonymously if that is the surest way to get candid responses. They can conduct focus groups to learn about employee feelings and attitudes toward their well-being and how they perceive the organization's impact on their well-being.

Step 5: Identify outside resources. Your health care provider and other community businesses and organizations may have excellent and inexpensive resources you can leverage. Take the best examples and practices from other nonprofits that match your organization's needs and adapt them to fit. Bring in experts to provide education and tools to help carry out your strategy.

Step 6: Establish your budget. Your organization can work creatively with partners, your health insurance vender, third-party vendors, and community organizations to devise—and even barter for—affordable activities and programs. The many nonprofits we interviewed for this book got creative with their workplace well-being activities and leveraged low-cost, free, and donated resources. Meka S. Sales, health program officer at the Duke Endowment, shared that the total annual budget for their program was $8,000. This included the costs of incentives, mostly gift cards for staff who won health challenges, and the cost of fresh fruit for snacks in the break room.

At some point, there will be unavoidable expenses associated with implementation. A lean budget should not be a deterrent to moving forward with your well-being initiatives. Take an incremental approach, and never stop looking for opportunities to fund raise and reallocate funds to help cover associated costs. Even a few small steps and changes in the right direction can have a tremendous impact and positive snowball effect.

WHY EMPLOYEE ENGAGEMENT IS ESSENTIAL

We cannot emphasize enough the importance of employee feedback and engagement to ensure the success of your Happy, Healthy Strategy. In all the interviews we did for this book, the common theme we heard from nonprofits with thriving WE-care cultures was that they engaged their employees from the beginning. The more involvement and feedback you get from in-house staff from the start, the better chances you'll have for profound and lasting success.

Your Happy, Healthy Committee is a critical employee engagement tool. When employees are engaged, they participate in programs and activities because they feel a sense of ownership and want to do so, not because they are required. They are passionate about participating and get more energy for their work. They share what they've learned and gained with others and encourage others to engage.

"Nine years ago our HR director established an employee committee to launch our program," says Sales. "The committee meets regularly, surveys staff, creates strategy, and helps steward the plan and evaluates the program." Their program is a blend of a traditional wellness program and other soft benefits.

In some cases, a committee is formed by an organization's director as a way of helping to put more permanent policies and programs in place. At the Crisis Response Network, a new executive director triggered a complete overhaul of the organization's culture, workplace, and policies. Justin Chase, LMSW, CPHQ, took an assessment of the staff's attitudes and performances at work and realized that a fundamental change had to happen. He took the time to listen to every employee, including the night shift staff, to hear their complaints firsthand and then addressed them.

Chase formed an employee engagement committee made up of people from different departments throughout the organization to report directly to him to turn complaints into concrete changes. He started small, addressing a complaint about dress code discrepancies between the daytime and nighttime staff. The committee was empowered to influence organization policies. It rewrote the dress code and added policy changes to allow staff to eat at their desks. Other changes also let everyone decorate and personalize their workstation, something previous management forbade.

Stepping up the changes, Chase proposed a room in the office be turned into anything the staff wanted as long as they used it for their purpose of choice. The committee created a survey using SurveyMonkey to get staff input and learned that a majority wanted a room with exercise equipment. The committee even polled the staff to find out the type of equipment they'd like in the room. The result was a well-used fitness facility that fosters a stronger sense of well-being among staff. Members of Crisis Response Network's employee engagement committee became the cheerleaders of the organization's well-being and wellness initiatives, and they continue to take the pulse of the staff to find out what else can be improved. They've also been empowered to carry out assessments, make environmental changes, and influence policy changes.

Foundation Center focuses on well-being in the workplace, something that came about when there was an opportunity for the organization to move into new office space. Says Jen Bokoff, director of knowledge services, "When you sign a long-term lease, it needs to be for a space where staff want to work and can be excited about, both for longevity and to help ease transition. The old office felt 'unenergized' and inefficient and had cockroaches in the stairwell." Definitely a deterrent for walking in the stairwells to promote exercising at work!

Bokoff said her organization wanted the new space to reflect more modern ways of working and communicating to keep staff excited about coming to work and to really make the space something they were proud of and comfortable spending time in.

"A committee of more than 20 people was put together to represent all teams. Everyone took their role on the committee very seriously and came to each meeting with questions, concerns, and ideas," recalls Bokoff.

Their committee not only discussed specific design features, such as an extra ladies bathroom, but they considered many wellness and well-being topics, such as the food in the vending machines and types of desks. They also discussed how the physical space of the workplace might influence cultural norms and improve social interaction, another element of well-being.

Says Bokoff, "The feedback on all fronts was varied and full of vivacious discussion. For every opinion, there was a counter opinion, and all were appreciated and logical. Decisions were ultimately made by a smaller 'executive move committee,' which was very helpful for keeping to a timeline. And we were able to integrate physical features that infuse well-being and wellness into our culture and the way we work."

As you can see, employee engagement is the fuel for your Happy, Healthy Strategy. Your employee engagement committee is the vehicle to drive that engagement.

Forming Your Employee Engagement Committee

Your employee engagement committee should be diverse. Include representation from different departments and recruit people with different skill sets. Consider bringing on people who fit one or more of the following:

- Someone from human resources to help craft the plan
- Someone from legal to review potential policy changes
- Someone with health expertise, if possible

- Someone with a disability to help develop suitable programs or program variations
- Someone with a strong interest or expertise in self-care or an existing self-care practice
- An events organizer and planner type
- Someone in a managerial position
- Someone in the trenches at the staff level
- Health insurance rep (optional)

Make sure to form a committee large enough to distribute duties equitably given everyone's already busy workload, but small enough to be nimble and efficient. Include your in-house Happy, Healthy Champions as part of your employee engagement committee; however, make sure your committee also consists of leaders and decision makers. You may need to "trickle up" buy-in, growing your committee with organization influencers over time. You have to start somewhere, so don't give up before you even begin just because you're hitting a wall with leadership.

Give your committee a name. It can be as simple as Happy Healthy Committee, Well-Being Committee, or Employee Engagement Committee, whatever works for your organization's culture. According to Amber Hacker of Interfaith Youth Core, their organization's committee is called the Giddy Committee, because they plan activities and programs that create community and social connection, an important aspect of well-being. Says Hacker, "This is a fantastic committee that gets feedback from all staff, and they have a lot of fun!"

As with any committee work, a statement of purpose can help guide the design and implementation of your Happy, Healthy Strategy. Project Harmony formed a Trauma-Informed Care Committee that supports the creation of and implementation of programs and policies to support the organization's well-being and wellness programs. It also surveyed staff through open forums and department check-ins. This is the statement that guided the committee:

> Everyone will know about the importance of staff self-care and everyone will have their own self-care plan.

Treat your Happy, Healthy Committee as you would any planning committee. Have clear roles and responsibilities, a well-thought out agenda, and a regular meeting schedule.

Getting Employee Feedback for Buy-In

For your Happy, Healthy Strategy to be successful, find out what your staff value. While surveys are great, if your organization isn't too large, an effective way to find out what employees really want is to ask them in one-on-one conversations. Ask simple questions such as, "What kind of well-being program could we offer here that would be meaningful for you?" and "What would it take to get you to actively participate and engage in a well-being initiative?" Remember that whatever programs you decide to set up as part of your plan, they must be relevant for individual employees as well as for the organization as a whole.

Says Duppins of DonorsChoose, "We are a very data-driven organization. We do a regular survey of staff on different well-being topics, and we use it as a quick way to get ideas about activities to pilot. We don't have the money to do everything that staff asks for, and that's why we implement programs and activities that staff really find most attractive and our committee will drive. Our approach is to listen when they ask for something new, and make it as easy as possible for people to take the lead on the activities that mean the most to them."

Amber Hacker of Interfaith Youth Core says they wanted staff feedback on their personnel policies—such as retirement benefits, parental leave, and flextime—all contributors to well-being. To better understand what staff cared about, they facilitated an "unconference" during a staff retreat to carry out unstructured dialogue and conversations. They received feedback on all of the policies that were subsequently integrated into their employee handbook.

Your organization's staff will respond best to well-being activities they help design and organize. Come up with creative and even fun ways to get feedback from staff about well-being programs that can inform your strategy. Make programs and initiatives stronger by changing existing or setting new policies to support them.

YOUR POLICIES AND EMPLOYEE BENEFITS

Part of your Happy, Healthy Strategy is to audit and review your organization's existing policies and employment benefits that are described in your employee handbook and other documents. Your policies and benefits should be in sync with your wellness and well-being programs and goals. Research and propose changes to existing policies as well as discuss any new policies that could be put into place to better reflect your organization's happier, healthier culture.

The nonprofit Idealist crafts its policies and benefits so staff have considerable discretion and as much flexibility as possible. The organization respects the variations and preferences of staff when trying to balance their professional and personal lives. Its policies reflect a belief that when staff members are healthy, supported, and have the flexibility they need, improvements occur in service quality, work effectiveness, and organizational climate. Says founder and executive director, Ami Dar, "Idealist is committed to investing in long-term staff stability and satisfaction while acknowledging that there is no one-size-fits-all formula for policies and benefits that create well-being."

Says, Kara Montermoso, HR manager at Idealist, "Staff benefits and policies like wellness, which include sabbaticals and vacation time, are broadly defined. We feel that many aspects can contribute to one's sense of well-being in the workplace, even if impacted by events or situations that are personal and not work-related. And though some benefits are industry standards, we do listen to staff feedback about how to make a particular program work most effectively. From a fiscal standpoint, we provide benefits that can be low-cost with high-impact or satisfaction, benefits that we know we can scale and/or sustain as we grow, and benefits that are competitive and/or reflect best practices."

You probably have a number of workplace policies already stated in your employee handbook including basic health-related policies such as a tobacco-free workplace, an alcohol/drug-free environment, safety and emergency procedures, and disaster preparedness. While you can't create organizational policies that dictate a person's personal lifestyle and habits, you can make statements about what your organization will do to encourage and support well-being through environmental changes, activities, cues, and resources. For example, you can set policies for what your nonprofit will pay for in terms of meals and snacks and the quality of the food purchased for all employees. You can have a policy stating that your organization will only pay for healthy snacks provided on-site for staff.

Another area where your organization can set policy is around work processes and how and when employees can and should break from work to encourage happier, healthier working habits. Jewish

Family & Children's Service of the Suncoast in Sarasota, Florida, staff deals with death and dying, chronic illness, and relationship and money issues on a daily basis with the aging population they serve. The organization offers generous time off policies to help support staff well-being: three weeks vacation the first year, four weeks vacation in all other years, up to 20 paid holidays per year, and one sick day per month.

When BJ Wishinsky, social media manager at Benetech, was volunteering at another nonprofit, she observed a virus—as in actual sickness—overtake one staff member after another because people kept coming into the office even when they were sick. When a job opened up at the nonprofit, Wishinsky thought carefully about working as a full-time employee at the organization.

Wishinsky recounts, "I asked the team, 'Do you have to be a masochist to work at a nonprofit, or does nonprofit work just tend to attract people who are self-sacrificing?'" That drew some laughter but also a realization that the organization needed to work on changing people's attitudes toward self-care—literally an attention to taking care of oneself when sick. Wishinsky says the organization eventually created a policy for staff to stay home when sick, and they (mostly) complied.

Softer Policies with Big Impacts

Can you create policies that guide human interactions at work, an important aspect of well-being? Yes, and Creating the Future did just that. "In 2014, we hired our first employee, and it came with making all the decisions that organizations so often boilerplate, including employment policies like sick time and paid time off," recalls Hildy Gottlieb, cofounder. "In September of 2014, our board began discussing those issues. I kicked off that conversation in a post for *Huffington Post* [titled] 'Kindness as Workplace Policy' and at our board meeting. We wanted to not simply talk about benefits as a budget item but think about the type of workplace we create and the conditions needed to support it. The result was a policy rooted in our humanity and in conversation."

See3, a digital agency working with nonprofits, put several policies in place that promote well-being and that affect the way its staff works and manages work-life issues. The agency doesn't count sick days or personal days, and it offers paid maternity and paternity leave policies, flexible schedule options, and work-from-home flexibility. See3 also has an office policy baked right into its employee handbook that allows employees to bring their dogs to work. Here's an excerpt:

> Dog-Friendly Office Policy
>
> The presence of dogs at See3 has been a unique and to some a treasured part of our workplace culture. Dogs can be a valued and important part of employees' lives and their ability to keep a dog at the workplace may enhance the quality of their work life.

The policy goes on in detail about being responsible, cleaning up after one's dog, the places that are off limits, what to do if there's an issue with another employee, and other finer details of canine presence at the office.

"There is loads of research out there about dogs reducing stress," says Michael Hoffman, the CEO. "It's also about work-life integration and balance. It was something that was important to me."

Project Harmony Child Protection Center has a mission to protect and support children, collaborate with professionals, and engage the community to end child abuse and neglect. Its staff encounters horrific cases of child abuse and neglect on a daily basis.

"It is very easy for staff to feel overwhelmed, burned out, and suffer from secondary trauma. It is very easy for them to forget their own well-being," says Gene Klein, executive director. To address employee stress, the organization brings a comfort dog into the office three days a week. It also provides wellness days and opportunities for staff to boost their morale and spirits.

Here's how Crisis Text Line in New York City talks about self-care in its employee handbook.

> Self-Care
>
> Lots of people talk about it. We actually do it. You make Crisis Text Line special. You are our most important asset. We need

you in tip-top shape! Self-care means identifying your own stress triggers and following a plan to keep them at bay. It means checking in with yourself on an ongoing basis. It means taking time to do things that make you happy. It means having a hobby that makes you feel full. It means snuggling with your dogs on a daily basis. We suggest creating a self-care plan and sharing it with your manager.

Here are some self-care tips from one of our staff and crisis counselors:

- Keep a self-care plan in sight. Seeing it means not forgetting about it.
- Walks. Fresh air. Nature.
- Take a digital break one day a week.
- Spend time with people you love.
- Always have a good book to get lost in.
- Coloring books (seriously. They're not just for kids. Proven to reduce stress!)

The above statements about self-care appear on page 6 of Crisis Text Line's employee handbook, front and center. That kind of prominence and acknowledgment of the importance of self-care sets the stage for all other rules, guidelines, and policies for the organization. Your Happy, Healthy Strategy succeeds through observed behaviors, open dialogue, concrete actions, and written policies, even for the softer perks and benefits.

Tech Policies for Tech Wellness

Technology within nonprofits is not being managed for the sake of people's health often enough. We've referenced stats and studies about tech addiction and the maladies our beloved tech gadgets and screens can cause us. Unhealthy tech habits can lead to mental, physical, and spiritual harm for individuals. Tech use needs to be addressed by organizations in employee handbooks, work policies, and wellness and well-being plans.

Noelle Chesley, associate professor of sociology at the University of Wisconsin–Milwaukee, looked at research around employers, workers, and tech use and found that workers and employers need to work together to figure out what technology-based practices are effective. Chesley says the onus of selecting healthy communication practices should be on the employer, which can then establish organizational policies around best practices.

Without written policies in place that address nonwork-hour tech use by staff, organizations may be unwittingly—or even knowingly—encouraging or supporting the bad habits that create a corporate culture of work without rest, relief, or downtime. While your organization can point fingers at individual workers and blame them for a lack of control over how and when they use their mobile devices, your organization needs to examine internal policies and attitudes toward mobile and tech use that erode boundaries between work life and home life.

You can get more information about policies you are allowed to set within your organization from the Equal Employment Opportunity Commission. There are federal rules pertaining to traditional wellness plans and health care benefits, so do your homework. Remember: We are not HR lawyers. Anytime you're implementing or changing work policy, check with your HR department and legal counsel.

WRITING YOUR HAPPY, HEALTHY STRATEGY

Your Happy, Healthy Committee can help bring together the different parts of your strategy and develop well-being policies, benefits, activities, and programs that best fit your organization and overall goals for less stress and less burnout. Here's a checklist of common components for your Happy, Healthy Strategy:

____ Purpose statement
____ List of committee members
____ Goals and objectives
____ Assessments
____ Assessment summary
    ____ Environmental assessments
    ____ Policy assessments
    ____ Cultural assessments
____ Employee surveys and focus groups

____ Benchmarks and baselines
____ Programs, activities, and cues
____ In-house education
____ Rewards and incentives
____ Physical workplace changes
____ Policies and policy changes
____ Well-being partners
____ Community resources
____ Coaching support
____ Peer-to-peer support
____ Group support
____ Online tools
____ Recommended apps
____ Internal communications plan
____ Evaluation

Rewards versus Penalties

While incentives can move your well-being programs forward, be careful not to penalize or even fire someone for not participating or for not doing well when participating. Check with your legal counsel to make sure you don't cross any lines or break any rules. Avoid rewards that encourage only one-time participation. Many of the programs focused on lifestyle changes actually require longer-term attention to habit change. Some research shows tying rewards to lifestyle change can potentially oversimplify the task and place too much focus on the reward, leading to shortcuts or even cheating.

After your staff has participated in surveys and assessments and provided input and feedback to your committee, everyone should feel invested in the launch of your well-being programs or activities, even anticipating them. You've identified everyone's areas of interest in terms of well-being and self-care, their current habits and practices, and even what types of changes they'd like to see or programs they'd like to have available at your organization. Tuning into staff and stakeholder needs and interests guides your committee to the right programs, policies, and perks that should be warmly received.

ROLLING OUT YOUR STRATEGY

Rolling out your strategy and introducing new programs or initiatives requires well-crafted educational information, messaging, and communications tools. As with any campaign that launches a new product or service, you need to provide some education to help people understand what you'll be revealing to them in the near future along with clear and easily accessible messaging. Take a multimedia approach to communicating your plan to reach employees multiple times and in a variety of ways.

Here are some ideas for getting early awareness and engagement leading up to your launch event:

- Run an organization-wide contest to come up with a name or slogan for the initiative.
- Solicit ideas for incentives and prizes that will stimulate participation.
- Order health-oriented products and merchandise with your organization's logo. Think T-shirts, pedometers, and water bottles.
- Get early sign-ups for an e-mail newsletter about personal and organizational self-care.
- Hang up posters around your office that attract attention and create interest.
- Make small environmental changes around the office that get noticed:
  - Improved lighting
  - Plants
  - Standing desks
- Add fitness and health-related items around the office space:
  - Healthy snacks
  - Fresh water
  - Exercise balls
  - Jump ropes

Marketing campaigns usually involve a slow build with teasers to help pique interest to get people talking about the upcoming announcement and asking questions early on. Use preliminary questions to help hone your messaging and programs and to better understand where staff might be misunderstanding or be resistant to your initiatives. Don't drag out the prep and teasers for your actual launch for too long. Capitalize on the interest and momentum and reveal your Happy, Healthy Strategy before people lose interest.

Developing Resource Materials

The materials you share at your organization to support your strategy rollout should tie personal self-care and WE-care directly to impact. Communicate the message that even the smallest changes toward healthier habits can create a positive ripple effect in each person's life to help him or her work more effectively on the organization's mission. Provide easy access to resource materials you develop or obtain.

Distribute a summary of your strategy in print and digital form as a PDF file. Other resources you can provide include:

- An easy-to-access library of resources on your company intranet or digital collaborative space containing related well-being materials, including videos, audio, and PDF files
- Revised copies of your employee handbook with relevant changes and additions regarding wellness and self-care
- Articles in an existing internal newsletter or other regular form of organization-wide communication, digital, print, or both
- E-mail invitations and reminders with regular tips and cues to keep self-care and well-being on everyone's minds

Contact your health insurance provider to see what resources it offers. Cigna, for example, provides an extensive online archive of materials including an audio and video library covering hundreds of wellness and well-being topics, a repository of articles with health and wellness tips, and a Healthy Balance Toolkit for customers to log into and take personal wellness assessments including one focused on stress. Don't only offer materials developed in-house but look to the vast landscape of wellness and well-being resources online and in your community and curate the content to best represent the spirit of your self-care and well-being initiatives.

Promoting Your Strategy

Plan a kickoff event to introduce your strategy to staff and generate excitement. Reinforce the message that staff is valued and that there is buy-in from leadership to foster a culture of well-being at your organization. At the launch, leadership should be well represented and provide statements to show support for and engagement with the plan and programs.

Some ways you can promote your strategy or programs and activities:

- Posters, flyers, table tents, stickers, magnets, and other display materials
- A calendar of well-being events and activities available in digital and print formats
- Computer screensavers
- Traditional mailings
- Paycheck inserts
- Organizational town hall meetings
- Physical bulletin boards in shared spaces and break rooms
- Bathroom stall signage
- Laminated wallet cards
- Workstation accessories like mouse pads or stress balls

Produce and disseminate objects and materials that act as visual cues to remind people of the well-being initiatives. Use both online and off-line materials to cover all the bases.

Once launched, provide training sessions to start the education process. Keep the momentum going by sharing success stories of self-care to celebrate individuals and groups embracing well-being, participating in programs, and experiencing positive results. Share results and give concrete examples of how putting the collective oxygen mask on your organization is producing better services and outcomes for the communities you serve. Create positive peer pressure within your organization where people are celebrated and rewarded when they participate in happier, healthier behaviors.

Build camaraderie and reinforce happy, healthy behaviors by encouraging staff participation in health-related events outside of your organization including health fairs, health assessments, sports or movement activities, and challenges like community walks and runs. The key is to give people options that fit their personalities, their needs, and their interests and to ensure everyone has at least some options that work for them.

Put out a call for new ideas and suggestions on a regular basis to give staff a sense of ownership of the programs. Reward the submission of new ideas that are adopted, and give credit when someone's idea is adopted.

Look for ways to surprise and delight staff on a regular basis. Integrate well-being into every aspect of your organization, across departments, and up and down organizational hierarchies. No one should be immune from the contagion of chronic self-care!

EVALUATING YOUR HAPPY, HEALTHY ORGANIZATION

Track the results of your organization's Happy, Healthy Strategy from the beginning. Andrew Means, cofounder of The Impact Lab, says, "When measuring a well-being initiative, it is often thought you can just ask someone about the unobservable thing you are trying to improve. For example, 'Are you feeling happy?'" Means says that kind of question doesn't provide good, reliable data. Means recommends looking at more tangible and observable outcomes and track those.

Create a well-being dashboard that is accessible to your board, director, staff, even volunteers, and, if relevant, funders. The most useful well-being dashboards measure both the employee and organization side through surveys, observations, and anecdotes with concrete numbers and statistics.

Employee	Organization
Engagement	Health-care spending
Satisfaction	Safety record
Well-being	Productivity (organization)
Productivity (individual)	Culture

Happy, Healthy Indicators

Health Indicators

- Program participation and attendance
- Biometric indicators improve
- Number of sick days used
- Health care costs

Productivity Indicators

- Employee job satisfaction scores
- Employee reviews
- Absenteeism rates
- Turnover rates
- Retention rates
- Buzz and referrals for new hires
- Internal promotions

Culture Indicators

- Employee comments from focus groups or conversations
- Employee survey that measures perceived sense of overall well-being (physical, emotional, social, financial, career, and community)
- Morale
- A feeling of humanity
- Clear sense of a higher purpose on an organizational and individual level

Revisit your assessments and outcomes at regular intervals. Compare progress to the baselines and celebrate successes. Check in with your board, director, and staff through evaluation surveys. Continue to chart progress in visible ways, sharing the data with all stakeholders and reviewing the bigger picture at the end of the year.

Keep in mind that your organization's well-being efforts are not all about the data. Data should serve as talking points to share stories of personal triumphs and observations and evidence of culture shifts and your happier, healthier environment. It is easy to get obsessed with the numbers or to feel that only numbers can properly express the ROI of your Happy, Healthy Strategy. Broaden your focus to acknowledge life-changing and life-saving results, enhanced work quality and work environment, and overall improved quality of life because of your happier, healthier organizational culture.

Take feedback to heart. Learn from mistakes and missteps and address what isn't working. Analyze why not. Don't bury failures under the proverbial rug, but speak openly about them and look for solutions with wide input. Don't play a blame-game pointing fingers, but instead encourage open and honest feedback and suggestions on how to improve your Happy, Healthy Strategy and programs.

SHOUT HALLELUJAH, COME ON GET HAPPY AND HEALTHY!

Being a Happy, Healthy Nonprofit means empowering your staff to thrive in life and at work. Doing so not only transforms your nonprofit into a high-performing organization but also an awesome place to work. If you follow the steps we've outlined in this book, you will create a never-ending well of vibrant and self-sustaining energy, passion, and excitement for your nonprofit's work that will positively affect outcomes. Be patient, persistent, and keep everyone's eyes on the prize: happier, healthier people; a happier, healthier nonprofit; and more impact without burnout!

Notes

INTRODUCTION

1. World Health Organization, "Self-care in the Context of Primary Health Care", Report of the Regional Consultation, Bangkok, Thailand, January 2009, http://www.searo.who.int/entity/primary_health_care/documents/sea_hsd_320.pdf.
2. Allison Fine, email interview with authors, February 2016.

CHAPTER 1

1. Joan Garry, "My Biggest Professional Mistake," www.joangarry.com/my-biggest-professional-mistake/.
2. Aisha Moore, About, *Self-Care by Aisha*, www.selfcarebyaisha.com/about-2/.
3. Cindy Leonard, "Tips for Managing Anxiety," April 14, 2016, www.cindyleonard.org/4-tips-for-managing-anxiety/.
4. Aspen Baker, *The Discipline of Self-Care*, Compasspoint, June 12, 2015, https://www.compasspoint.org/blog/discipline-self-care.
5. Mike Belmares, "Tackling Work Life Balance in the Nonprofit Sector," Idealist Careers, June 4, 2014, http://idealistcareers.org/tackling-work-life-balance-in-the-nonprofit-sector/.
6. "Stressed Out by Work? You're Not Alone," Knowledge @ Wharton, University of Pennsylvania, October 20, 2014, http://knowledge.wharton.upenn.edu/article/stressed-work-youre-alone/.
7. Herbert Freudenberger, https://en.wikipedia.org/wiki/Herbert_Freudenberger.
8. Robert L. Veninga and James P. Spradley, *The Work/Stress Connection: How to Cope with Job Burnout* (Boston, MA: Little Brown & Co, 1981).
9. C. Maslach, M. P. Leiter, and S. E. Jackson, "Making a Significant Difference with Burnout Interventions: Researcher and Practitioner Collaboration," *Journal of Organizational Behavior* 33 (2012): 296–300 [published online October 12, 2011, doi: 10.1002/job.784]
10. Sherrie Bourg Carter, "The Tell Tale Signs of Burnout ... Do You Have Them?" *Psychology Today*, November 26, 2013, https://www.psychologytoday.com/blog/high-octane-women/201311/the-tell-tale-signs-burnout-do-you-have-them.
11. Arianna Huffington, "Burnout: Time to Abandon a Very Costly Collective Delusion," *Huffington Post*, June 6, 2014, www.huffingtonpost.com/arianna-huffington/burnout_b_5102468.html.
12. Sherry E. Sullivan, Monica L. Forret, Shawn M. Carraher, and Lisa A. Mainiero, "Using the Kaleidoscope Career Model to Examine Generational Differences in

Work Attitudes," Fairfield University, January 1, 2009, http://digitalcommons.fairfield.edu/cgi/viewcontent.cgi?article=1057&context=business-facultypubs.

13. Universum, *Millenials: A Six-Part Series*, http://universumglobal.com/millennials/.
14. Ann Goggins and Don Howard, "The Nonprofit Starvation Cycle," *Stanford Social Innovation Review*, Fall 2009, http://ssir.org/articles/entry/the_nonprofit_starvation_cycle.
15. "Nonprofit Overhead Cost Project," August 2004, https://philanthropy.iupui.edu/files/research/nonprofit_overhead_brief_3.pdf.
16. Rusty Morgen Stahl, M.A., "Talent Philanthropy: Investing in Nonprofit People to Advance Nonprofit Performance," www.talentphilanthropy.org/wp-content/uploads/2013/10/Talent-Philanthropy-Article-in-Fdn-Rvw.pdf (October 2013).
17. Ira Hirschfield, "Less Than One Percent: Why Leadership Development Should Be a Core Part of Grantmaking," Haas Jr., September 11, 2014, www.haasjr.org/perspectives/less-than-one-percent.
18. Marissa Tirona, phone interview with author, February 2016.
19. American Psychological Association, "Stress in the Workplace," https://www.apa.org/news/press/releases/phwa-survey-summary.pdf (March 2011).
20. "Executive Director Listening Project," Meyer Foundation, http://meyerfoundation.org/news-room/publications/executive-director-listening-project.
21. Monisha Kapila, "The Business Case for Investing in Talent," *Stanford Social Innovation Review*, May 7, 2014, http://ssir.org/articles/entry/the_business_case_for_investing_in_talent.
22. Lori Bartczak, "Combatting Burnout in Nonprofit Leaders," *Stanford Social Innovation Review*, May 21, 2014, http://ssir.org/articles/entry/combatting_burnout_in_nonprofit_leaders.
23. American Psychological Association, "Stress in the Workplace," https://www.apa.org/news/press/releases/phwa-survey-summary.pdf (March 2011).
24. A. E. Dembe, J. B. Erickson, R. G. Delbos, S. M. Banks, "The impact of overtime and long work hours on occupational injuries and illnesses: new evidence from the United States". *Occupational & Environmental Medicine*, 62:9 (2005): 588–597, http://oem.bmj.com/content/62/9/588.full.
25. Sarah Green Carmichael, "The Research Is Clear: Long Hours Backfire for People and for Companies," *Harvard Business Review*, August 19, 2015, https://hbr.org/2015/08/the-research-is-clear-long-hours-backfire-for-people-and-for-companies.
26. Sarah Green Carmichael, "Working Long Hours Makes Us Drink More," *Harvard Business Review*, April 10, 2015, https://hbr.org/2015/04/working-long-hours-makes-us-drink-more.
27. Rob Beschizza, "Productivity Slumps after 40–50 Hours of Work a Week," Boingboing, August 21, 2015, http://boingboing.net/2015/08/21/productivity-slumps-after-40-5.html.
28. United Nations High Commissioner for Refugees, "Staff Well-Being and Mental Health in UNHCR", 2016, http://www.unhcr.org/56e2dfa09.pdf.
29. Mark Horvath, email interview with authors, February 2016.
30. N. Owen, A. Bauman, and W. Brown, "Too Much Sitting: A Novel and Important Predictor of Chronic Disease Risk?" *British Journal of Sports Medicine*, December 2, 2008, http://bjsm.bmj.com/content/43/2/81.full.

31. Nilofer Merchant, "Got a Meeting? Take a Walk," TED, February 2013, https://www.ted.com/talks/nilofer_merchant_got_a_meeting_take_a_walk?language=en.
32. "Stressed Out by Work? You're Not Alone," Knowledge @ Wharton, Wharton University of Pennsylvania, October 20, 2014, http://knowledge.wharton.upenn.edu/article/stressed-work-youre-alone/.
33. Lee Rainie and Kathryn Zickuhr, "Chapter 1: Always on Connectivity," Pew Research Center Internet, Science & Tech, August 26, 2015, www.pewinternet.org/2015/08/26/chapter-1-always-on-connectivity/.
34. Brandon T. McDaniel and Sarah M. Coyne, "'Technoference': The Interference of Technology in Couple Relationships and Implications for Women's Personal and Relational Well-Being," *Psychology of Popular Media Culture* 5, no. 1 (January 2016): 85–98. doi:10.1037/ppm0000065.
35. Beth Kanter, "7 Tips To Help You Focus in Age of Distraction: Are You Content Fried!" *Beth's Blog*, September 29, 2012, www.bethkanter.org/distraction-focus/.
36. Beth Kanter, "How to Train Your Attention and Be Effective When Working Online," *Beth's Blog*, September 15, 2014, www.bethkanter.org/gold-fish-attention/.
37. Linda Stone, "Continuous Partial Attention," http://lindastone.net/qa/continuous-partial-attention/.

CHAPTER 2

1. Aisha Moore, *Self-Care by Aisha*, www.selfcarebyaisha.com/2014/08/05/the-Self-Care-bill-of-rights/.
2. "Our Self-Care Starter Kit," University at Buffalo, https://socialwork.buffalo.edu/resources/self-care-starter-kit.html.
3. "Insufficient Sleep Is a Public Health Problem," Centers for Disease Control and Prevention, www.cdc.gov/features/dssleep/.
4. Maria Popova, "Happy Birthday, Brain Pickings: 7 Things I Learned in 7 Years of Reading, Writing, and Living", *Brain Pickings*, https://www.brainpickings.org/2013/10/23/7-lessons-from-7-years/.
5. Arianna Huffington, *Sleep Revolution: Transforming Your Life, One Night at a Time*, (New York: Harmony Books, 2016).
6. "National Sleep Foundation's Sleep Time Duration Recommendations: Methodology and Results Summary," *Sleep Health Journal of the National Sleep Foundation*, March 2015, www.sleephealthjournal.org/article/S2352-7218%2815%2900015-7/fulltext.
7. "Combating Stress with a Balanced Nutritional Diet," Stress Management Society, www.stress.org.uk/files/combat-nutritional-stress.pdf.
8. Aviroop Biswas, Paul I. Oh, Guy E. Faulkner, Ravi R. Bajaj, Michael A. Silver, Marc S. Mitchell, and David A. Alter, "Sedentary Time and Its Association with Risk for Disease Incidence, Mortality, and Hospitalization in Adults: A Systematic Review and Meta-analysis," *Annals of Internal Medicine*, 162(2):123–132, http://annals.org/article.aspx?articleid=2091327.
9. "Physical Activity Reduces Stress," Anxiety and Depression Association of America, www.adaa.org/understanding-anxiety/related-illnesses/other-related-conditions/stress/physical-activity-reduces-st.

10. American Psychological Association, *Stress in America*, 2014, http://www.apa.org/news/press/releases/stress/2014/snapshot.aspx.
11. "2008 Physical Activities Guidelines for Americans," U.S. Department of Health and Human Services, http://health.gov/paguidelines/pdf/paguide.pdf.
12. "Are Communications about Work Outside Regular Working Hours Associated with Work-to-Family Conflict, Psychological Distress and Sleep Problems?" *Work & Stress: An International Journal of Work, Health & Organisations* 27, no. 3 (2013), www.tandfonline.com/doi/pdf/10.1080/02678373.2013.817090.
13. "Work-Home Interference Contributes to Burnout" , *Journal of Occupational and Environmental Medicine*, April 11, 2014, http://www.ishn.com/articles/98351-work-home-interference-contributes-to-burnout.
14. "Charts from the American Time Use Survey," United States Department of Labor, www.bls.gov/tus/charts/.
15. ETEC 510 contributors, "Social Media Anxiety Disorder," ETEC510, February 7, 2015, http://etec.ctlt.ubc.ca/510wiki/index.php?title=Social_Media_Anxiety_Disorder&oldid=62282.
16. Larry Rosen, *iDisorder: Understanding Our Obsession with Technology and Overcoming Its Hold on Us,* (New York: St. Martin's Press, 2012).
17. Russell B. Clayton, Glenn Leshner, and Anthony Almond, "The Extended iSelf: The Impact of iPhone Separation on Cognition, Emotion, and Physiology," *Journal of Computer-Mediated,* 2015, 20(2): 119–135.

CHAPTER 3

1. "Is Your Lifestyle Causing You Stress?" School of Social Work, University at Buffalo, https://socialwork.buffalo.edu/content/dam/socialwork/home/self-care-kit/lifestyle-behaviors.pdf.
2. "Self Care Assessment," Crisis Text Line, https://online.crisistextline.org/sites/default/files/Self_Care_Assessment.pdf.
3. Charles Duhigg, *The Power of Habit: Why We Do What We Do in Life and Business,* (New York: Random House, 2012).
4. Gretchen Rubin, *Better Than Before: Mastering the Habits of Our Everyday Lives,* (New York: Crown Publishing Group, 2015).
5. Jason Hreha, "Models to Know: Fogg Behavior Model," Big Think, http://bigthink.com/wikimind/models-to-know-fogg-behavior-model.
6. Daniel H. Pink, *Drive: The Surprising Truth About What Motivates Us* (New York: Riverhead Books, 2009).
7. BJ Fogg, "How to Change," Tiny Habits, http://tinyhabits.com/.
8. BJ Fogg, "Join Me," Tiny Habits, http://tinyhabits.com/join/.
9. Gretchen Rubin, "My New Book about Habit Formation, as Distilled in 21 Sentences," July 9, 2014, http://gretchenrubin.com/happiness_project/2014/07/my-new-book-about-habit-formation-as-distilled-in-21-sentences/.

CHAPTER 4

1. Lolly Daskal, "Success Is A Sunrise Away," Lolly Daskal Lead From Within, http://www.lollydaskal.com/leadership/success-is-a-sunrise-away/ (December 1, 2015).
2. Iren Tankova, Ana Adan, and Gualberton Buela-Casal, "Circadian Typology and Individual Differences: A Review," *Personality and Individual Differences* 16, no. 5 (July 1994): 671–684, https://www.researchgate.net/publication/223442402_Circadian_typology_and_individual_differences_a_review_Personality_and_Individual_Differences_16_671-684.
3. Kimberly A. Aikens et al., "Mindfulness Goes to Work: Impact of an Online Workplace Intervention," *Journal of Occupational & Environmental Medicine* 56, no. 7 (July 2014): 721–731, http://journals.lww.com/joem/Abstract/2014/07000/Mindfulness_Goes_to_Work__Impact_of_an_Online.7.aspx.
4. Brain & Spine Team, "3 Reasons Adult Coloring Can Actually Relax Your Brain," Cleveland Clinic, November 13, 2015, http://health.clevelandclinic.org/2015/11/3-reasons-adult-coloring-can-actually-relax-brain/.
5. Shai Coggins, *Today: Life: A Guided Journal on Everyday Moments,* (Adelaide, South Australia: Paper Boat Publishing, 2015).
6. Jane E. Brody, "The Health Benefits of Knitting," Personal Health, *New York Times*, January 25, 2016, http://well.blogs.nytimes.com/2016/01/25/the-health-benefits-of-knitting/?_r=0.

CHAPTER 5

1. Daniel Goleman, *Emotional Intelligence: Why It Can Matter More than IQ,* (New York: Bantam Books, 1995.)
2. Daniel Goleman, "How Emotionally Intelligent Are You?" http://www.danielgoleman.info/daniel-goleman-how-emotionally-intelligent-are-you/ (April 21, 2015).
3. Marie Kondo, *The Life-Changing Magic of Tidying Up: The Japanese Art of Decluttering and Organizing*, (New York: Ten Speed Press, 2014).
4. Marie Kondo, *Spark Joy: An Illustrated Master Class on the Art of Organizing and Tidying Up*, (New York: Ten Speed Press, 2016).
5. Peter Bregman, *18 Minutes: Find Your Focus, Master Distraction, and Get the Right Things Done,* (New York: Business Plus, 2011).
6. Brian Tracey, *Eat That Frog!: 21 Great Ways to Stop Procrastinating and Get More Done in Less Time* (San Francisco, CA: Berrett-Koehler Publishers, 2006).
7. Tony Schwartz, Jean Gomes, and Catherine McCarthy, *The Way We're Working Isn't Working: The Four Forgotten Needs That Energize Great Performance,* (New York: Free Press, 2011).
8. Alan Hedges, Cornell University, http://ergo.human.cornell.edu/CUESitStandPrograms.html.
9. Sheena Greer, "Ludo: How Play Can Transform Your Work," *Pamela's Grantwriting Blog*, http://pamelasgrantwritingblog.com/12Days2015/LUDOeBook.2015.pdf.

10. Howard Rheingold, "Infotention Skills: From Information Overload to Knowledge Navigation," Howard Rheingold University, www.rheingold.com/university/pages/infotention-webinar.php.
11. Pang, Alex Soojung-Kim, *The Distraction Addiction: Getting the Information You Need and the Communication You Want, Without Enraging Your Family, Annoying Your Colleagues, and Destroying Your Soul* (New York: Little, Brown and Company, 2013).
12. Daniel J. Levitin, *The Organized Mind: Thinking Straight in the Age of Information Overload,* (New York: Dutton, 2014).
13. "A Provisional Guide for Observing a Weekly Day of Rest," Sabbath Manifesto, www.sabbathmanifesto.org/.

CHAPTER 6

1. Josh Levine, "Get the Culture Code," CultureLabx, http://culturelabx.com/culture -code/.
2. Karen Kent, Ron Z. Goetzel, Enid C. Roemer, Aishwarya Prasad, Naomi Freundlich, "Promoting Healthy Workplaces by Building Cultures of Health and Applying Strategic Communications", *Journal of Occupational & Environmental Medicine*, February 2016, 58(2): 114–122, http://journals.lww.com/joem/Abstract/2016/02000/Promoting_Healthy_Workplaces_by_Building_Cultures.2.aspx.
3. "Workplace Genome," WorkXO, www.workxo.com/genome.
4. Carter McNamara, "Organizational Culture and Changing Culture," Free Management Library, http://managementhelp.org/organizations/culture.htm.
5. "Stressed Out by Work? You're Not Alone," Knowledge at Wharton, Wharton University of Pennsylvania, http://knowledge.wharton.upenn.edu/article/stressed-work-youre-alone/.
6. "The State of the American Workplace: Employee Engagement Insights for U.S. Business Leaders," http://employeeengagement.com/wp-content/uploads/2013/06/Gallup-2013-State-of-the-American-Workplace-Report.pdf (June 2013).
7. "Strategies for Changing Your Organization's Culture," The Bridgespan Group, http://www.bridgespan.org/Publications-and-Tools/Leadership-Effectiveness/Lead-and-Manage-Well/Strategies-for-Changing-Organizations-Culture.aspx".
8. Laura Putnam, *Workplace Wellness that Works: 10 Steps to Infuse Well-Being and Vitality into Any Organization,* (Hoboken, NJ: Wiley, 2015).
9. Julie Rogers and Joshua Bernstein, "Meyer Releases 2013 Open Letter to the Community," October 29, 2013, http://meyerfoundation.org/meyer-releases-2013-open-letter-community.
10. Peter F. Drucker, *The Ecological Vision: Reflections on the American Condition* (New Brunswick, NJ: Transaction Publishers, 1993).
11. Anese Cavanaugh, *Contagious Culture: Show Up, Set the Tone, and Intentionally Create an Organization that Thrives*, (New York: McGraw-Hill Education, 2015).
12. Bryce Williams, "Wellness Support: Peer-to-Peer = Results!" Blue Shield of California, https://www.blueshieldca.com/sites/documents/calpershbo/news/Peer_Support_A45513_2-13.pdf.

13. Gretchen Rubin, "Why Joining a Habits Group Can Help You Change Your Habits—and How to Start One," January 15, 2016, http://gretchenrubin.com/happiness_project/2016/01/habits-group-can-help-you-change-your-habits/.
14. "Science Behind Peer Support," Peers for Progress, http://peersforprogress.org/learn-about-peer-support/science-behind-peer-support/.

CHAPTER 7

1. Jennifer Goldschmied et al., "Napping to Modulate Frustration and Impulsivity: A Pilot Study," *Personality and Individual Differences* 86 (November 2015): 164–167, www.sciencedirect.com/science/article/pii/S0191886915003943.
2. Sara C. Mednick et al., "Comparing the Benefits of Caffeine, Naps and Placebo on Verbal, Motor, and Perceptual Memory," Take a Nap!, http://saramednick.com/htmls/pdfs/Mednick_BBR_08%5B8%5D.pdf.
3. "Be Trendy: Sleep at Work!" The Sleep Hub, September 25, 2015, http://thesleephub.com/trendy-sleep-work/.
4. "Nap Desks Are the Newest Way to Recharge at Work!" MyGunnedah, www.mygunnedah.com.au/nap-desks-are-the-newest-way-for-you-to-recharge-at-work/.
5. "Napping Office Chair," Fancy, https://fancy.com/things/950810569613514450/Napping-Office-Chair?ref=pink1976.
6. "Position Statement on Financial Incentives within Worksite Wellness Programs," American Heart Association, https://www.heart.org/idc/groups/heart-public/@wcm/@adv/documents/downloadable/ucm_428966.pdf.
7. "StairWELL to Better Health," Centers for Disease Control and Prevention, www.cdc.gov/physicalactivity/worksite-pa/toolkits/stairwell/index.htm.
8. Lydia Dishman, "8 Top Office Design Trends for 2016," *Fast Company*, December 18, 2015, www.fastcompany.com/3054804/the-future-of-work/8-top-office-design-trends-for-2016.
9. Joshua Sharpe, "911 Operators Exercising During Calls," *Gwinnett Daily Post*, March 9, 2016, www.gwinnettdailypost.com/local/cities/lawrenceville/operators-exercising-during-calls/article_d43a0461-e29d-530c-9a7f-d53c7194da25.html.
10. Robert I. Sutton, *The No Asshole Rule: Building a Civilized Workplace and Surviving One That Isn't* (New York: Warner Business Books, 2007).
11. "Code Lavender Program Receives National Recognition," North Hawaii Community Hospital, September 24, 2015, https://www.nhch.com/cms/Static/News.aspx?id=223.
12. "What is Mindfulness-Based Stress Reduction?," Mindful Living Programs, http://www.mindfullivingprograms.com/whatMBSR.php.
13. Randi Zuckerberg, "Make Time to Be Creative, Especially If It's in Your 'Discomfort Zone,'" LinkedIn, February 8, 2016, https://www.linkedin.com/pulse/my-life-outside-work-make-time-creative-especially-its-zuckerberg.
14. "GoodWellness Resource Guide: A Step Up Program for a Happier and Healthier You," Goodwill Manasota, 2015, http://www.goodwillsewcareers.com/rewards.

CHAPTER 8

1. Beth Kanter, "How One Nonprofit Senior Staff Uses Walks and Talks," *Beth's Blog*, November 5, 2015, www.bethkanter.org/walk-talk/.
2. "Flex at a Glance Brochure," When Work Works, http://gorowe.com/pages/about-rowe.
3. "Who We Are," Results-Only Work Environment, www.gorowe.com/what-we-do-1/.
4. Stacy Kono, "The Nonprofit Four-Day Workweek: You Can Take Care of Yourself and Still Change the World," *Rockwood Leadership Institute Blog*, January 13, 2015, http://blog.rockwoodleadership.org/nonprofit-four-day-workweek-can-take-care-still-change-world/.
5. Rick Nauert, "Leisure Play Is Important for Human Collaboration," PsychCentral, April 17, 2009, http://psychcentral.com/news/2009/04/17/leisure-play-is-important-for-human-collaboration/5398.html.
6. Jared Keller, "The Psychological Case for Adult Play Time," Pacific Standard, https://psmag.com/the-psychological-case-for-adult-play-time-701755406fee#.63h2erq8u (April 99, 2015).
7. Mervyn Humpherys, interview with author, January 2016.
8. "The Office at World Wildlife Fund," The Muse, https://www.themuse.com/companies/worldwildlifefund/office.
9. Aria Finger (CEO, Do Something), interview with author, January 2016.
10. "Working for Mind," Mind, www.mind.org.uk/about-us/working-for-us/.
11. Deborah S. Linnell, Tim Wolfred PsyD, "Creative Disruption: Sabbaticals for Capacity Building & Leadership Development in the Nonprofit Sector," The Durfee Foundation, 2009, http://durfee.org/wp-content/uploads/Creative-Disruption-Sabbatical-Monograph.pdf.
12. Dennis McMillian, "What I Did That You Should Consider," The Foraker Group, https://www.forakergroup.org/index.php/resources/presidents-letter/what-i-did-that-you-should-consider/.
13. The Geraldine R. Dodge Foundation, "Sabbaticals Matter," *Dodge Blog*, October 12, 2015, http://blog.grdodge.org/2015/10/12/sabbaticals-matter/#sthash.INqt9hZY.dpbs.
14. Dennis McMillian, "Burnout," The Foraker Group, http://www.forakergroup.org/index.php/resources/presidents-letter/burnout/.

CHAPTER 9

1. "2015 Employer Health Benefits Survey," The Henry J. Kaiser Family Foundation, September 22, 2015, http://kff.org/report-section/ehbs-2015-section-twelve-health-risk-assessment-biometrics-screening-and-wellness-programs/.
2. Soeren Mattke, Hangsheng Liu, John P. Caloyeras, Christina Y. Huang, Kristin R. Van Busum, Dmitry Khodyakov, and Victoria Shier, *Workplace Wellness Program Study: Final Report*, Rand Corporation, 2013, http://www.rand.org/pubs/research_reports/RR254.html.
3. Tom Rath and Jim Harter, "The Five Essential Elements of Wellbeing," *Gallup Business Journal*, May 4, 2010, www.gallup.com/businessjournal/126884/Five-Essential-Elements-Wellbeing.aspx.

Index

Q

R

S

T

U

V

W

Y

Z